BATCH BUT BETTER

TO MY MOOMIN MAMA, FOR EVERYTHING.

AN HACHETTE UK COMPANY
WWW.HACHETTE.CO.UK

FIRST PUBLISHED IN GREAT BRITAIN IN 2016
AS *THE BOUNTIFUL KITCHEN* BY KYLE BOOKS,
AN IMPRINT OF OCTOPUS PUBLISHING GROUP LIMITED
CARMELITE HOUSE
50 VICTORIA EMBANKMENT
LONDON EC4Y 0DZ
WWW.KYLEBOOKS.CO.UK

THIS EDITION PUBLISHED IN 2021

10 9 8 7 6 5 4 3 2 1

ISBN: 978 0 85783 946 6

DISTRIBUTED IN THE US BY HACHETTE BOOK GROUP, 1290
AVENUE OF THE AMERICAS, 4TH AND 5TH FLOORS, NEW YORK,
NY 10104

DISTRIBUTED IN CANADA BY CANADIAN MANDA GROUP, 664
ANNETTE ST., TORONTO, ONTARIO, CANADA M6S 2C8

A CATALOGUING IN PUBLICATION RECORD FOR THIS TITLE IS
AVAILABLE FROM THE BRITISH LIBRARY

EDITOR **VICKY ORCHARD**
DESIGN **HELEN BRATBY**
PHOTOGRAPHY **LAURA EDWARDS**
ILLUSTRATION **CLAIRE HARRUP**
FOOD STYLING **LIZZIE KAMENETZKY**
PROPS STYLING **POLLY WEBB-WILSON**
PRODUCTION **GEMMA JOHN AND NIC JONES**

PRINTED AND BOUND IN CHINA

BATCH
BUT
BETTER

3 MEALS FROM 1

LIZZIE KAMENETZKY
PHOTOGRAPHY BY LAURA EDWARDS

KYLE BOOKS

CONTENTS

INTRODUCTION

I adore leftovers. A fridge full of bits and bobs, small bowls of saved deliciousness, ready to be turned into something wonderful. The hard work has been done; now you can reap the rewards.

The sad thing is that, as a word, 'leftovers' sounds so humble and unloved. It tends not to be a word to excite passion and get the heart racing. It speaks of dishes made out of desperation, of can't-quite-be-bothered-ness and of reheating tired ingredients from the day before. Once you realize the full potential, the freedom and fun you can have with a little left over from a wonderful meal, how you cook will be revolutionized.

The way we shop has a lot to do with why people are not embracing leftovers. Shopping to cook a different meal every night of the week not only risks ingredients sitting in your fridge unused until they perish, but also that when you have leftovers they end up being thrown away, ironically because you have something planned for the next day that you don't want to waste.

The *Batch but Better* way of cooking is thrifty, flexible and good for the bank balance, the planet and your skills as a ready-for-anything cook. We are all busy and it might seem scary not to have fully planned your meals. But once you break away from over-shopping, you will feel such relief that you'll never go back.

Of course, you still need to plan a bit. As much as I love the idea of eternal leftovers, the reality is that, in order to have leftovers, you need to cook. For three or four nights of the week, plan to cook something delicious, then experiment with the wonderful leftovers and some fridge raiding for the rest of the week! The key to those days when you open your fridge to investigate what you might have to turn into something tasty for supper does rely on one thing. The store cupboard. People bang on about store cupboard suppers, and then they ask you to have all manner of weird and wonderful ingredients that, in reality, you may never have unless you either love them or buy them specially.

Fridge-raid cooking produces some of my most creative and wonderful dishes, almost entirely by a mix of happy accident and necessity. I hope you will love this book as much as I enjoyed writing it and be inspired to discover your own leftover favourites.

STORE + FRIDGE

This is not an exhaustive list of all the useful things you can have in your cupboard and fridge to help change the way you cook, but it is a good place to start.

SIMPLE SPICES
Cumin seeds, coriander seeds, dried chilli flakes, star anise, fennel seeds, cinnamon sticks, ground turmeric, paprika, cardamom pods

TINS
Tomatoes, chickpeas, beans, lentils, coconut milk, tuna

PACKET AND BOX
Eggs, basmati rice, risotto rice, pasta, noodles, grains

FLAVOUR BOOSTERS
Tomato purée, mustards, anchovies, olives, horseradish, harissa, capers, cornichons, stock cubes

BOTTLES
Olive oil, vinegars, soy sauce, Worcestershire sauce, ketchup, mayonnaise, Tabasco sauce

BAKING
Flours, caster sugar, brown sugar, vanilla extract, raisins or sultanas/dried fruit, ground almonds and other nuts, oats, stem ginger, maple syrup, golden syrup, yeast, chocolate

IN THE DARK
Onions, shallots, garlic, potatoes/parsnips/celeriac, fresh tomatoes

ON THE SILL
Lemon/lime/orange, pots of growing herbs – basil, thyme, parsley, tarragon, rosemary, chives

CHILLED
Butter, milk, cream/cream cheese/yogurt/crème fraîche, bacon/pancetta/chorizo, hot-smoked salmon or mackerel, cheese such as Parmesan/Gruyère/blue cheese/feta/Cheddar/goat's, greens such as cabbage/broccoli/sprouts/kale, courgette/aubergine, salad and leaves, ginger and chillies

DEEP FREEZE
Peas, beans, puff pastry, ice cream, frozen berries, fresh breadcrumbs, frozen prawns

SPROUTING BROCCOLI, SHERRY + ALMONDS
BAKED EGGS WITH SPROUTING BROCCOLI
GIANT COUSCOUS + SPROUTING BROCCOLI

BAKED BEETROOT WITH SOURED CREAM + HERBS
BEETROOT PILAF
BEETROOT + FETA CAKE

SCANDI POTATO SALAD
POTATO SALAD ROASTIES
FRITTATA

BRAISED RED CABBAGE
RED CABBAGE CHUTNEY
MIXED PICKLED BRASSICA SLAW

ROAST AUBERGINE + TOMATOES
PASTA BAKE WITH AUBERGINE + TOMATOES
AUBERGINE + TOMATO MINI CALZONES

ROOT VEGETABLE GRATIN
GRATIN HASH WITH POACHED EGGS
SAVOURY GRATIN MUFFINS

BEST EVER TOMATO SAUCE
VEGGIE RISSOLES IN TOMATO SAUCE
POTATO + HALLOUMI IN SPICED TOMATO SAUCE

SPRING VEGETABLE + RICOTTA SALAD
SALAD FRY-UP
GREEN DIP

BAKED SQUASH WITH CHILLI + ROSEMARY
SQUASH + PARMESAN SOUFFLÉ
SQUASH LASAGNE

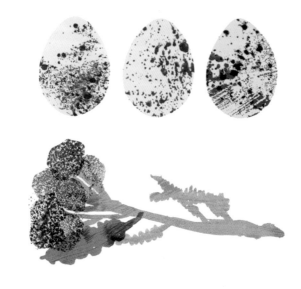

VEGETABLES

Broccoli doesn't need to be boring. The little trees are great absorbers of flavour and dressings. This would be a fantastic side dish for a roast or griddled chicken breast, but I think it would also make a fantastic simple lunch.

SPROUTING BROCCOLI, SHERRY + ALMONDS

SERVES 4 AS A SIDE, PLUS LEFTOVERS
5 MINUTES TO MAKE
15 MINUTES TO COOK

OLIVE OIL, TO FRY

3 BANANA SHALLOTS, FINELY SLICED

500G (1LB 2OZ) SPROUTING BROCCOLI

75ML (5 TABLESPOONS) SHERRY, SUCH AS OLOROSO OR MANZANILLA

SEA SALT AND FRESHLY GROUND BLACK PEPPER

50G (1¾OZ) BLANCHED ALMONDS, TOASTED

EXTRA VIRGIN OLIVE OIL, TO SERVE

1. Heat a good layer of oil in a non-stick frying pan and gently fry the shallots for 10 minutes until golden and crisp. Drain on kitchen paper.

2. Stand the broccoli in a deep pan with about 5cm of boiling water, cover and cook for 5-6 minutes until the stems are tender.

3. Meanwhile, heat 1 tablespoon of oil in a pan and add the cooked broccoli, then splash in the sherry. Season and scatter with the almonds and crispy shallots. Drizzle with extra virgin olive oil to serve.

ENOUGH LEFT OVER FOR:
BAKED EGGS WITH SPROUTING BROCCOLI (PAGE 12)
GIANT COUSCOUS + SPROUTING BROCCOLI
    (PAGE 14) »———→

Eggs are such a useful ingredient to help turn humble leftovers into fabulous suppers!

BAKED EGGS WITH SPROUTING BROCCOLI

SERVES **4**

10 MINUTES TO MAKE

30 MINUTES TO COOK

1 TABLESPOON OLIVE OIL

1 LARGE ONION, FINELY SLICED

2 GARLIC CLOVES, CRUSHED

400G (14OZ) CAN OF CHOPPED
  TOMATOES

SEA SALT AND FRESHLY GROUND BLACK
  PEPPER

200G (7OZ) LEFTOVER SPROUTING
  BROCCOLI, SHERRY + ALMONDS
  (PAGE 11)

150G (5½OZ) EXTRA BITS, SUCH AS
  CHOPPED BACON, CHORIZO, SALAMI
  OR SMOKED SALMON OR MACKEREL
  (OPTIONAL)

4 FREE-RANGE EGGS

1. Preheat the oven to 180°C/fan 160°C/350°F/gas 4. Heat the oil in an ovenproof non-stick frying pan and fry the onion for 10 minutes until softened. Add the garlic and fry for 30 seconds, then add the tomatoes. Season and bubble for 10 minutes.

2. Chop the leftover broccoli into small pieces and add to the pan. If you have any other bits to add, then chuck them in (you can crisp up any meaty bits first if you like).

3. Make four little wells in the mixture and crack an egg into each one, then pop into the oven and bake for 8-10 minutes until the eggs are set but the yolks are still soft.

tip If you don't have any leftover broccoli, then you can either quickly make the Sprouting Broccoli, Sherry + Almonds (page 11) or simply blanch 200g (7oz) sprouting or tenderstem broccoli instead.

A great portable lunch or picnic dish, just toss it all together, pack up and go.

GIANT COUSCOUS + SPROUTING BROCCOLI

SERVES 4
5 MINUTES TO MAKE
5 MINUTES TO COOK

200G (7OZ) GIANT COUSCOUS OR
  COUSCOUS, BULGUR WHEAT OR A
  SMALL PASTA LIKE FREGOLA
500ML (18FL OZ) HOT VEGETABLE OR
  CHICKEN STOCK (PAGE 101)
200G (7OZ) LEFTOVER SPROUTING
  BROCCOLI, SHERRY + ALMONDS
  (PAGE 11)
SHAVINGS OF PARMESAN CHEESE
  OR ANY OTHER CHEESE, SUCH AS
  FETA, PECORINO, GOAT'S CHEESE OR
  BLUE CHEESE
JUICE OF 1 LEMON
SEA SALT AND FRESHLY GROUND BLACK
  PEPPER
PINCH OF DRIED CHILLI FLAKES
  (OPTIONAL)
EXTRA VIRGIN OLIVE OIL, TO DRIZZLE

1. Gently simmer the giant couscous in the hot stock for 5–6 minutes until tender. Roughly chop the broccoli and put into a bowl. Drain the couscous, toss in with the broccoli and add any bits of cheese you may have. Squeeze in the lemon juice to taste, add some seasoning and chilli flakes if you want, drizzle with olive oil and serve.

tip Without making the Sprouting Broccoli, Sherry + Almonds (page 11), simply blanch 200g (7oz) sprouting or tenderstem broccoli before making this recipe. You can add a splash of sherry vinegar too if you have it.

Beetroot with its lovely earth flavour needs very little adornment. It loves an aniseed flavour so dill and tarragon are particular friends of the sweet beet.

BAKED BEETROOT WITH SOURED CREAM + HERBS

SERVES **4**, PLUS LEFTOVERS
10 MINUTES TO MAKE
40 MINUTES TO COOK

1KG (2LB 4OZ) SMALL OR MEDIUM
  BEETROOT, SCRUBBED AND CUT INTO
  WEDGES
2 TABLESPOONS OLIVE OIL
1 TEASPOON CUMIN SEEDS
SEA SALT AND FRESHLY GROUND BLACK
  PEPPER
100ML (3½FL OZ) SOURED CREAM
A HANDFUL OF CHOPPED DILL
A HANDFUL OF CHOPPED FLAT-LEAF
  PARSLEY
50G (1¾OZ) CHOPPED TOASTED
  WALNUTS

1. Preheat the oven to 200°C/fan 180°C/400°F/gas 6. Tumble the beetroot into a roasting tin and toss with the olive oil and cumin seeds. Season and roast for 40 minutes until tender.

2. Stir through the soured cream with a splash of warm water, add the herbs and spoon into a dish. Sprinkle with the chopped walnuts and serve.

tip Toast the walnuts in a dry frying pan or in the oven for 4 minutes at 160°C/fan 140°C/325°F/gas 3 until golden. Watch very carefully as they will burn very quickly.

ENOUGH LEFT OVER FOR:
BEETROOT PILAF (PAGE 18)
BEETROOT + FETA CAKE (PAGE 20) ⇥⟶

Ever versatile, a pilaf is the perfect way to breathe new life into your leftovers. I would tend to choose rice over pasta as my go-to store cupboard staple, its tender grains feel lighter and more nourishing when you are looking for a quick, simple supper.

SERVES **4**
5 MINUTES TO MAKE
15 MINUTES TO COOK

250G (9OZ) LONG GRAIN RICE
SEA SALT AND FRESHLY GROUND BLACK
   PEPPER
1 TABLESPOON OLIVE OIL
1 LARGE ONION, FINELY CHOPPED
200G (7OZ) GREENS, SLICED (ANY GREEN
   LEAFY VEG WOULD WORK WELL)
300-350G (10½-12OZ) LEFTOVER BAKED
   BEETROOT WITH SOURED CREAM
   + HERBS (PAGE 17), ROUGHLY
   CHOPPED
100-200G (3½-7OZ) ANY EXTRA BITS YOU
   HAVE, SUCH AS SMOKED FISH, GOAT'S
   CHEESE, LEFTOVER CHICKEN OR
   LAMB (OPTIONAL)
A HANDFUL OF FINELY CHOPPED FLAT-
   LEAF PARSLEY
LEMON JUICE, TO TASTE

BEETROOT PILAF

1. Cook the rice in boiling salted water for 15 minutes until tender.

2. Meanwhile, heat the oil in a pan and fry the onion for 10 minutes until soft and lightly golden. Drain the rice and add to the pan and toss in the fried onion.

3. Blanch the greens briefly in boiling water, then drain and add to the rice with the leftover beetroot and any other bits you have. Season and add the parsley and lemon juice to taste and serve.

tip Grate 150g (5½oz) beetroot and gently fry in a little butter and splash of stock or water until tender, then add to your pilaf if you don't have any leftover Baked Beetroot (page 17).

The Scandi flavours of the Baked Beetroot with Soured Cream + Herbs (page 17) work strangely well with Greek feta, which is another lover of aniseed – think chilled glasses of ouzo in the warm Aegean sunshine with sharp and tangy feta salads.

BEETROOT + FETA CAKE

SERVES **4**
10 MINUTES TO MAKE
15 MINUTES TO COOK

ABOUT 250G (9OZ) LEFTOVER BAKED
   BEETROOT WITH SOURED CREAM
   + HERBS (PAGE 17)
400G (14OZ) CAN OF CHICKPEAS OR
   BUTTER BEANS, DRAINED AND
   RINSED
200G (7OZ) FETA, CRUMBLED
2 TABLESPOONS GRAM OR PLAIN
   FLOUR
1 FREE-RANGE EGG
SEA SALT AND FRESHLY GROUND BLACK
   PEPPER
A HANDFUL OF FLAT-LEAF PARSLEY,
   FINELY CHOPPED
SUNFLOWER OIL, FOR FRYING

1. Whizz the beetroot and chickpeas together in a food processor to form a rough paste. Transfer to a bowl and add the feta, flour and egg and mix well. Season and mix in the parsley.

2. Heat a layer of oil in a 20–22cm (8–8½in) non-stick frying pan and spoon the mixture into the pan and flatten. Fry for 3–4 minutes until a golden crust has formed. Turn over with a spatula – in quarters if it starts to break up. Fry for a further 3–4 minutes, then serve piping hot.

tip If you haven't cooked the Baked Beetroot with Soured Cream + Herbs (page 17) then grate about 200g (7oz) raw beetroot and mix with a dollop of soured cream and some chopped dill. This would also be wonderful served with a fried or poached egg.

A good potato salad recipe is something that everyone should have in their arsenal. This one is so much more than just a side, full of delicious pickles and onions it's a wonderful meal in itself.

SERVES **4**, PLUS LEFTOVERS
15 MINUTES TO MAKE
15 MINUTES TO COOK

SCANDI POTATO SALAD

1 SMALL RED ONION, FINELY SLICED

1 TABLESPOON RED WINE VINEGAR

1KG (2LB 4OZ) NEW POTATOES

SEA SALT AND FRESHLY GROUND BLACK
   PEPPER

½ CUCUMBER, DESEEDED AND FINELY
   DICED

1 BUNCH OF SPRING ONIONS, FINELY
   SLICED

5–6 LARGE DILL PICKLES, FINELY SLICED

2 TEASPOONS DIJON OR ENGLISH
   MUSTARD

4 TABLESPOONS SOURED CREAM

2 TABLESPOONS MAYONNAISE

2 TABLESPOONS GREEK OR NATURAL
   YOGURT

A HANDFUL OF DILL, FINELY CHOPPED

1. Put the onion in a little bowl, pour over the vinegar and set aside.

2. Put the potatoes in a pan of cold, salted water and bring to the boil, then simmer for 12–15 minutes until tender. Drain and slice in half or quarter if large.

3. Tip the potatoes into a bowl and add the remaining ingredients. Season well and serve warm or at room temperature scattered with the red onion.

ENOUGH LEFT OVER FOR:
POTATO SALAD ROASTIES (PAGE 24)
FRITTATA (PAGE 25) ⇒⟶

When thinking about fun things to do with leftover potato salad, the thought struck me that it could be fun to try roasting it up. It seemed like a bonkers idea but the result was wonderful! Tender and crunchy with a tangy flavour from the rest of the ingredients.

SERVES **4**
5 MINUTES TO MAKE
1 HOUR TO COOK

POTATO SALAD ROASTIES

400G (14OZ) LEFTOVER SCANDI POTATO
   SALAD (PAGE 21)
2 TABLESPOONS OLIVE OIL
150G (5½OZ) RASHERS OF STREAKY
   BACON OR PANCETTA, CHOPPED

1. Preheat the oven to 200°C/fan 180°C/400°F/gas 6. Tip the leftover potato salad into a roasting tin, drizzle with the oil and roast for 30 minutes. Turn and scatter with the bacon bits and roast for a further 25–30 minutes until all is crispy.

tip If you haven't made the Scandi Potato Salad (page 21), cook 400g (14oz) new potatoes and toss with olive oil and a good tablespoon each of mayonnaise and Greek or natural yogurt and a few chopped pickled gherkins or cornichons before roasting.

Eggs make the best quick supper and are a great foil for lots of different flavours, so a frittata is one of the most satisfying simple dishes you can cook on a shoestring.

SERVES **4** AS A LUNCH
10 MINUTES TO MAKE
15 MINUTES TO COOK

FRITTATA

6 FREE-RANGE EGGS

250G (9OZ) LEFTOVER SCANDI POTATO SALAD (PAGE 21)

100–150G (3½–5½OZ) CHEESE, SUCH AS FETA, MOZZARELLA, PARMESAN OR RICOTTA, CRUMBLED OR GRATED IF NECESSARY

A HANDFUL OF CHOPPED FLAT-LEAF PARSLEY

SEA SALT AND FRESHLY GROUND BLACK PEPPER

A LITTLE OLIVE OIL OR BUTTER

1. Whisk the eggs in a bowl. Slice up the leftover potato salad and add to the bowl with the cheese and parsley. Season well.

2. Preheat the grill to medium. Gently heat a smidge of oil or butter in a 20–23cm (8–9in) non-stick frying pan over a low heat and pour in the mixture. Cook for 12–15 minutes until just set, then pop the pan under the grill for 30 seconds to golden up the top. Serve warm or at room temperature.

tip Without any leftover Scandi Potato Salad (page 21), cook 250g (9oz) new potatoes until tender, drain and toss with a dollop of mayonnaise and a dollop of Greek or natural yogurt and some olive oil. Add a few sliced gherkins or cornichons and a little bit of Dijon mustard, then leave to cool, before continuing as above.

Braised cabbage is not just for Christmas, take comfort in the slow-cooking process as crunchy vibrant raw cabbage gently mellows and sweetens as it becomes tender in the pot.

SERVES **4**, PLUS LEFTOVERS
5 MINUTES TO MAKE
1-1½ HOURS TO COOK

BRAISED RED CABBAGE

1 RED ONION, FINELY SLICED

1 LARGE RED CABBAGE, FINELY SLICED,
  CORE REMOVED

1 DESSERT APPLE, QUARTERED, CORED,
  PEELED AND GRATED

3 TABLESPOONS SOFT LIGHT BROWN
  SUGAR

60ML (4 TABLESPOONS) RED WINE
  VINEGAR, CIDER VINEGAR OR
  MALT VINEGAR

125ML (4FL OZ) DRY CIDER OR APPLE
  JUICE

1 CINNAMON STICK

SEA SALT AND FRESHLY GROUND BLACK
  PEPPER

1. Put all the ingredients into a large, heavy-based pan or flameproof casserole dish with a lid. Add a splash of water and bring to a simmer. Reduce the heat as low as possible and cook, covered, for 1–1½ hours until the cabbage is really tender, stirring occasionally. Season and serve.

ENOUGH LEFT OVER FOR:
RED CABBAGE CHUTNEY (PAGE 28)
MIXED PICKLED BRASSICA SLAW (PAGE 30) ⟩——→

A good chutney like this is worth its weight in gold for the transformation it makes to a plate of bread and cheese.

MAKES **2** x **400**ML
(**14**FL OZ) JARS
15 MINUTES TO MAKE
45 MINUTES TO COOK

RED CABBAGE CHUTNEY

ABOUT 400G (14OZ) LEFTOVER BRAISED
 RED CABBAGE (PAGE 27)
2 APPLES, SUCH AS COX, GRATED
A HANDFUL OF DRIED FRUIT, SUCH
 AS APRICOTS, PRUNES, SULTANAS OR
 RAISINS, CHOPPED IF LARGE
1 TEASPOON EACH YELLOW MUSTARD
 SEEDS, GROUND TURMERIC, CUMIN
 SEEDS AND DRIED CHILLI FLAKES
100G (3½OZ) PRESERVING SUGAR
175ML (6FL OZ) RED WINE VINEGAR

1. Put all the ingredients into a heavy-based pan, bring to a simmer and cook for 30–45 minutes until thickened and fragrant. Spoon into warm, sterilized jars and seal. Mature for a week in a cool, dark place before using. Once opened, keep in the fridge.

tips If you don't have the leftover Braised Red Cabbage (page 27), simply start with about 400g (14oz) raw cabbage instead and cook for an extra 20–30 minutes.

To sterilize your jars, wash well in hot soapy water, rinse, then put in a low oven (110°C/fan 90°C/225°F/gas ¼) to completely dry out. Or you could just put them on a hot wash in your dishwasher.

There is something really pleasing about the mix of textures in this slaw, where crunchy gives way to soft and yielding.

SERVES **4**

10 MINUTES TO MAKE,
PLUS MARINATING

200–250G (7–9OZ) LEFTOVER BRAISED
  RED CABBAGE (PAGE 27)
500G (1LB 2OZ) OTHER BRASSICAS,
  SUCH AS WHITE CABBAGE, POINTY
  CABBAGE, SAVOY CABBAGE OR KALE,
  FINELY SLICED
2 CARROTS, CUT INTO THIN LONG
  MATCHSTICKS
1 APPLE, SUCH AS COX, PEELED AND
  COARSELY GRATED
100ML (3½FL OZ) CIDER VINEGAR
50G (1¾OZ) CASTER SUGAR
1 TABLESPOON YELLOW MUSTARD
  SEEDS
2–3 TABLESPOONS SOURED CREAM,
  GREEK OR NATURAL YOGURT
EXTRA VIRGIN OLIVE OIL, TO DRIZZLE

MIXED PICKLED BRASSICA SLAW

1. Mix the leftover red cabbage with the other vegetables and apple in a large bowl and set aside. Heat the vinegar with the sugar and mustard seeds over a low heat until the sugar has melted. Pour the hot vinegar over the vegetables and toss together. Set aside for 20 minutes, then add the soured cream or yogurt and some extra virgin olive oil and seasoning and serve.

tip If you don't have any leftover Braised Red Cabbage (page 27), you can either make this recipe with 300g (10½oz) sliced raw red cabbage or fry the cabbage in a little butter with a good splash of cider and a little vinegar for 10–15 minutes until softened slightly.

One of my favourite dishes has to be aubergine parmigiana, but I was feeling a bit lazy and the thought of frying up aubergines and making sauce was a bit more than I felt like doing. So here is my quick version, all the flavour and the oven does all the work.

SERVES 4, PLUS LEFTOVERS
5 MINUTES TO MAKE
50 MINUTES TO COOK

ROAST AUBERGINE + TOMATOES

3 AUBERGINES, CUT INTO CHUNKS

300G (10½OZ) VINE TOMATOES, HALVED

1 BULB GARLIC, CLOVES SEPARATED

OLIVE OIL

SEA SALT AND FRESHLY GROUND BLACK PEPPER

2 BALLS BUFFALO MOZZARELLA, TORN

BASIL LEAVES, TO SCATTER

CRUSTY BREAD, TO SERVE

1. Preheat the oven to 180°C/fan 160°C/350°F/gas 4. Put the aubergines and tomatoes into a roasting tin and scatter in the garlic cloves. Drizzle with lots of olive oil and season well.

2. Roast for 40–45 minutes, turning the aubergine occasionally, until the aubergine is really tender and the tomatoes are soft and golden. Dot the mozzarella all over and return to the oven for 5–10 minutes. Scatter with basil and serve with crusty bread.

ENOUGH LEFT OVER FOR:
PASTA BAKE WITH AUBERGINE + TOMATOES (PAGE 32)
AUBERGINE + TOMATO MINI CALZONES (PAGE 33) ⟶

Sometimes it is the simplest things that are the most satisfying, showing that good food doesn't have to be complicated.

300G (10½OZ) SHORT PASTA, SUCH AS
   FUSILLI, PENNE OR RIGATONI
SEA SALT
1 TABLESPOON OLIVE OIL
1 ONION, FINELY SLICED
A GOOD PINCH OF DRIED CHILLI
   FLAKES OR 1 RED OR GREEN CHILLI,
   FINELY CHOPPED
300G (10½OZ) LEFTOVER ROAST
   AUBERGINE + TOMATOES (PAGE 31)
400G (14OZ) CAN CHOPPED TOMATOES
SPLASH OF CREAM, CRÈME FRAÎCHE
   OR SOURED CREAM
40G (1½OZ) PARMESAN CHEESE OR ANY
   OTHER MELTING CHEESE, SUCH AS
   COMTÉ, GRUYÈRE, FONTINA,
   TALEGGIO OR BRIE
A HANDFUL OF FLAT-LEAF PARSLEY,
   CHOPPED

PASTA BAKE WITH AUBERGINE + TOMATOES

1. Preheat the oven to 200°C/fan 180°C/400°F/gas 6. Cook the pasta in a pan of boiling salted water according to the packet instructions until almost but not quite cooked.

2. Meanwhile, heat the oil in a pan and gently fry the onion and chilli for 10 minutes until softened. Add the leftover aubergine and tomatoes and the canned tomatoes and simmer for 15-20 minutes. Add the cream, crème fraîche or soured cream, cheese and parsley, then tip the whole lot into an ovenproof dish and bake for 20-25 minutes until the top is golden.

tip If you haven't made the Roast Aubergine + Tomatoes (page 31), simply fry up an aubergine, sliced or chopped, in olive oil until really soft. Add a squidge of tomato purée to boost the tomato-ey flavour. Tear up a ball of mozzarella and toss through the pasta with the aubergine.

Making your own pizza dough is not only really easy, but great fun and tastes so much better than any pizza you can buy.

500G (1LB 2OZ) STRONG WHITE BREAD
FLOUR, PLUS EXTRA TO DUST
7G (¼OZ) SACHET FAST-ACTION DRIED
YEAST
2 TEASPOONS SEA SALT
2 TABLESPOONS EXTRA VIRGIN OLIVE
OIL
250G (9OZ) CAN CHOPPED TOMATOES
300G (10½OZ) LEFTOVER ROAST
AUBERGINE + TOMATOES (PAGE 31)
200G (7OZ) CHEESE, SUCH AS
PARMESAN, MOZZARELLA, BLUE
CHEESE OR A MIX
ANY OTHER STORE CUPBOARD
ADDITIONS, SUCH AS A COUPLE OF
ANCHOVIES, BLACK OLIVES OR
ARTICHOKE HEARTS

AUBERGINE + TOMATO MINI CALZONES

1. Mix the flour with the yeast and salt in a bowl. Add the oil and enough lukewarm water to form a soft but not too sticky dough. Knead vigorously for 10 minutes, then put the dough in a clean, oiled bowl and cover with clingfilm. Leave to rise in a warm place for an hour or until doubled in size.

2. Meanwhile, heat a pan until really hot, add the canned tomatoes and bubble for 5 minutes to reduce to a thick sauce. Add the leftover aubergine and tomatoes and bubble together for 10 minutes. Remove from the heat and set aside to cool.

3. Remove the dough from the bowl, knead briefly, then divide into 12 equal-sized balls. Preheat the oven to its hottest setting.

4. Roll and stretch each ball of dough to a disc about 16–18cm (6¼–7in) in diameter on a floured surface. Dollop a generous spoon of the aubergine into the middle, scatter with cheese and any other store cupboard additions you want. Brush the edges of the dough with water, fold in half and seal with a little twist, like a Cornish pasty.

5. Slide on to 1–2 baking sheets, then bake for 10–12 minutes until golden and crisp on the outside.

tip If you haven't cooked the Roast Aubergine + Tomatoes (page 31), dice an aubergine, drizzle with plenty of olive oil and roast for 30 minutes until soft. Use this with an extra squidge of tomato purée instead of the leftovers.

There was a bit of debate when photographing this recipe about the difference between a gratin and a dauphinoise. We reached the conclusion that a dauphinoise is a type of gratin and that anything topped with a browned crust is all 'familie gratin'.

ROOT VEGETABLE GRATIN

SERVES **4**, PLUS LEFTOVERS
15 MINUTES TO MAKE
1½ HOURS TO COOK

30G (1OZ) UNSALTED BUTTER

1 ONION

300G (10½OZ) FLOURY POTATOES

2 PARSNIPS

1 CELERIAC

A HANDFUL OF THYME SPRIGS, LEAVES
  STRIPPED

2 TABLESPOONS PLAIN FLOUR

SEA SALT AND FRESHLY GROUND BLACK
  PEPPER

300ML (10FL OZ) CHICKEN (PAGE 101)
  OR VEGETABLE STOCK

400ML (14FL OZ) DOUBLE CREAM

A HANDFUL OF FRESH OR DRIED
  BREADCRUMBS

50G (1¾OZ) CHEDDAR CHEESE, GRATED

1. Preheat the oven to 180°C/fan 160°C/350°F/gas 4. Rub the butter all over the inside of a 1.2-litre (2-pint) ovenproof dish. Peel and finely slice all the vegetables and toss together with the thyme, flour and plenty of seasoning. Tumble into the dish.

2. Mix the stock and cream together and pour over the vegetables, then mix the breadcrumbs and cheese together and scatter over the top. Bake for 1½ hours until the vegetables are tender and the top is golden and bubbling.

ENOUGH LEFT OVER FOR:
GRATIN HASH WITH POACHED EGGS (PAGE 36)
SAVOURY GRATIN MUFFINS (PAGE 38) »——→

I don't know what it is about a hash that is so completely satisfying and glorious – I think it is because I love anything that I can eat without a knife! This comforting, creamy hash is a true winter wonder.

GRATIN HASH WITH POACHED EGGS

SERVES **4**

20 MINUTES TO MAKE

25 MINUTES TO COOK

1 TABLESPOON OLIVE OIL

1 ONION, FINELY CHOPPED

100G (3½OZ) BACON, CHORIZO OR
 SALAMI, FINELY CHOPPED

2 GARLIC CLOVES, CRUSHED

400G (14OZ) LEFTOVER ROOT
 VEGETABLE GRATIN (PAGE 35)

A HANDFUL OF SOFT HERBS, SUCH
 AS FLAT-LEAF PARSLEY, TARRAGON
 OR BASIL, CHOPPED

4 FREE-RANGE EGGS

SEA SALT AND FRESHLY GROUND BLACK
 PEPPER

1. Heat the oil in a frying pan and gently fry the onion for 10 minutes until softened. Add the bacon and fry for 10 minutes until it is starting to crisp. Add the garlic and cook for 30 seconds, then add the leftover gratin and herbs, crushing slightly with a fork to flatten the gratin in the base of the pan.

2. Cook over a medium-low heat for 5–6 minutes until golden and brown on the bottom, then turn over with a spatula – don't worry if it breaks up a bit, just squash it back down again. Cook for a further 5–6 minutes until the other side is golden.

3. Meanwhile, bring a pan of water to the boil, then reduce the heat until the water is just simmering. Poach the eggs gently for 4 minutes.

4. Serve scoops of the hash with the softly poached eggs, plenty of freshly ground black pepper and a scattering of sea salt.

tips Without the leftover Root Vegetable Gratin (page 35) you can make a slightly different version of this hash. Peel and dice a potato, parsnip and a chunk of celeriac. Simmer in boiling water for a few minutes until tender, then drain. Add to the pan and fry up when you would fry the gratin, adding a splash of double cream as you go.

Remember the best poached eggs are made from the freshest ones, so go for ones as straight from the hen as you can!

A savoury gratin muffin is so much more versatile than the sweet kind. A fabulous breakfast on the go or a simple lunch warm from the oven with a glass of cold beer or cider.

SAVOURY GRATIN MUFFINS

MAKES **12**
15 MINUTES TO MAKE
18 MINUTES TO COOK

350G (12OZ) LEFTOVER ROOT VEGETABLE GRATIN (PAGE 35)

5 MEDIUM FREE-RANGE EGGS, SEPARATED

150G (5½OZ) SELF-RAISING FLOUR

60ML (4 TABLESPOONS) WHOLE MILK

30G (1OZ) UNSALTED BUTTER, MELTED

100G (3½OZ) GRATED CHEESE, SUCH AS CHEDDAR, PARMESAN OR GRUYÈRE

1 BUNCH OF CHIVES OR SPRING ONIONS, FINELY CHOPPED

1. Preheat the oven to 200°C/fan 180°C/400°F/gas 6 and line a 12-hole muffin tin with paper cases.

2. Mash the leftover gratin with a fork. Whisk the egg yolks and flour together, then whisk in the milk and add the mashed gratin, melted butter, cheese and chives or spring onions.

3. Whisk the egg whites in a clean bowl until holding stiff peaks, then gently fold them into the gratin mixture until just combined. Divide between the muffin cases and bake for 15–18 minutes until risen and golden. Leave to cool in the tin, then serve warm.

tip If you don't have any leftover Root Vegetable Gratin (page 35), peel and grate a small potato, a small parsnip and a little piece of celeriac. Blanch briefly in boiling salted water, then drain well and pat dry. Mix with a splash of double cream and plenty of seasoning and use 300g (10½oz) of this mixture instead of the leftover gratin.

So often tomato sauces are thin and watery or too sharp and raw-tasting. The key is in the roasting, the tomatoes slow cook and start to dry out, becoming sweeter and more intense before you turn them into the best tomato sauce you have ever tasted.

BEST EVER TOMATO SAUCE

SERVES **4**, PLUS LEFTOVERS
10 MINUTES TO MAKE
1 HOUR **10** MINUTES TO COOK

1.5KG (3LB 5OZ) RIPE VINE TOMATOES, HALVED
60ML (4 TABLESPOONS) OLIVE OIL, PLUS EXTRA TO DRIZZLE
SEA SALT AND FRESHLY GROUND BLACK PEPPER
3 GARLIC CLOVES, FINELY SLICED
2 TEASPOONS SHERRY VINEGAR
PINCH OF CASTER SUGAR

1. Preheat the oven to 200°C/fan 180°C/400°F/gas 6. Place the tomatoes in a large roasting tin, drizzle with a little olive oil and season with plenty of sea salt and freshly ground black pepper. Roast for 30–40 minutes.

2. Heat the remaining 60ml (4 tablespoons) oil in a saucepan, add the garlic and infuse very gently over a low heat for a minute, then set aside.

3. Once the tomatoes are really soft and tender, add them to the infused oil. Heat gently, crushing the tomatoes with a fork. Add the vinegar and sugar and bubble for 20–30 minutes until you have a thick, rich sauce.

4. Serve with freshly cooked pasta and lots of grated Parmesan.

ENOUGH LEFT OVER FOR:
VEGGIE RISSOLES IN TOMATO SAUCE (PAGE 42)
POTATO + HALLOUMI IN SPICED TOMATO SAUCE
(PAGE 43) ⇥⟶

I love the word rissole, it's so wonderfully old-fashioned, and these are lovely little fried balls of goodness smothered in a deliciously rich tomato sauce.

SERVES **4**
5 MINUTES TO MAKE
15 MINUTES TO COOK

300G (10½OZ) GRATED COURGETTES OR
    A MIX OF COURGETTES, CARROTS,
    POTATOES OR OTHER VEGETABLES
2 FREE-RANGE EGGS, BEATEN
1 SMALL ONION, RED ONION OR A FEW
    SPRING ONIONS, FINELY CHOPPED
8 TABLESPOONS PLAIN FLOUR
250G (9OZ) MIXED GRATED CHEESE,
    SUCH AS PARMESAN, CHEDDAR,
    FETA, MOZZARELLA OR GRUYÈRE
SEA SALT AND FRESHLY GROUND BLACK
    PEPPER
SUNFLOWER OIL, TO FRY
200–300ML (7–10FL OZ) LEFTOVER BEST
    EVER TOMATO SAUCE (PAGE 41)
A HANDFUL OF SOFT HERBS, SUCH
    AS BASIL, PARSLEY OR TARRAGON,
    CHOPPED

VEGGIE RISSOLES IN TOMATO SAUCE

1. Mix the grated vegetables with the eggs, onion, plain flour and cheese and some seasoning. Shape into 10 little balls.

2. Heat a little oil in a non-stick frying pan and fry the rissoles for 5–6 minutes until golden and crisp. Warm the leftover tomato sauce in a saucepan over a medium heat, add the rissoles, then bubble for a minute, scatter with the herbs and serve.

tip Without the leftover Best Ever Tomato Sauce (page 41) you can make a quick version. Heat a pan over a high heat and add a 400g (14oz) can of cherry tomatoes so that they splutter and fizz. Mash up and add a little splash of water and plenty of seasoning and cook for 10–15 minutes until thickened and reduced. Add a good glug of extra virgin olive oil, 1–2 teaspoons of red wine vinegar and a finely sliced garlic clove and simmer for a further minute or two.

Squeaky cheese is an apt name for this semi-soft Cypriot cheese, which bounces and squeaks delightfully between the teeth as it starts to cool. It has a wonderful sharp flavour which goes perfectly with the leftover Best Ever Tomato Sauce (page 41).

POTATO + HALLOUMI IN SPICED TOMATO SAUCE

SERVES 4
15 MINUTES TO MAKE
20 MINUTES TO COOK

1 TABLESPOON SUNFLOWER OIL
1 RED ONION, FINELY CHOPPED
1 CHILLI, FINELY CHOPPED OR
   1 TEASPOON DRIED CHILLI FLAKES
300-400ML (10-14FL OZ) LEFTOVER
   BEST EVER TOMATO SAUCE (PAGE 41)
500G (1LB 2OZ) NEW POTATOES, SWEET
   POTATOES OR SQUASH, SLICED OR
   CUT INTO CHUNKS
200G (7OZ) FROZEN PEAS, BROAD
   BEANS OR EDAMAME
225G (8OZ) HALLOUMI, PANEER,
   KEFALOTYRI OR KASSERI CHEESE,
   THICKLY SLICED INTO 8 PIECES
A HANDFUL OF SOFT HERBS, BASIL,
   FLAT-LEAF PARSLEY OR TARRAGON,
   CHOPPED

1. Heat the sunflower oil in a non-stick pan and gently fry the onion and chilli for 10 minutes until lovely and soft. Add the tomato sauce, a splash of water and the sliced potatoes or squash and simmer gently, covered, for 15–20 minutes until the potatoes or squash are completely tender. Add the peas and simmer for a further minute or two.

2. Heat a separate pan over a high heat and fry the slices of cheese for 1–2 minutes, turning once, until golden on both sides.

3. Stir the herbs through the potatoes/squash. Serve the fried cheese with the potatoes/squash and sauce.

tip Without the leftover Best Ever Tomato Sauce (page 41) you can make a quick version of the sauce. Heat a pan over a high heat and add a 400g (14oz) can of cherry tomatoes so that they splutter and fizz. Mash up and add a little splash of water and plenty of seasoning and cook for 10–15 minutes until thickened and reduced. Add a good glug of extra virgin olive oil, 1–2 teaspoons of red wine vinegar and a finely sliced garlic clove and simmer for a further minute or two.

I don't hold truck with anyone who tries to say that a salad is not filling or a meal in itself, after all, a salad is simply a collection of ingredients tossed together with a dressing, so anything goes and this one is packed full of all the wonderful flavours of spring.

SERVES 4, PLUS LEFTOVERS
15 MINUTES TO MAKE
15 MINUTES TO COOK

SPRING VEGETABLE +RICOTTA SALAD

300G (10½OZ) JERSEY ROYALS OR OTHER
  NEW POTATOES
12 SPEARS ASPARAGUS
150G (5½OZ) PODDED PEAS
150G (5½OZ) PODDED BABY BROAD
  BEANS
150G (5½OZ) RADISHES, HALVED
400G (14OZ) MIXED LETTUCES AND
  LEAVES, SUCH AS COS, BUTTER,
  RADICCHIO, ROCKET AND
  WATERCRESS, TORN
150G (5½OZ) FIRM RICOTTA, CRUMBLED

FOR THE DRESSING
JUICE OF 1 LEMON
2 TEASPOONS DIJON MUSTARD
½ TEASPOON CLEAR HONEY
SEA SALT AND FRESHLY GROUND BLACK
  PEPPER
5 TABLESPOONS EXTRA VIRGIN
  OLIVE OIL

1. Put the potatoes in a pan of cold, salted water, bring to the boil and simmer for 15 minutes or until tender. Drain, thickly slice and tip into a bowl.

2. For the dressing, whisk the lemon juice with the mustard and honey and plenty of seasoning, then whisk in the olive oil. Pour half the dressing over the warm potatoes.

3. Blanch the asparagus, peas and broad beans in boiling water for a couple of minutes, then drain and cool under cold running water. Slice the asparagus and remove the outer skins from the broad beans, then add both to the potatoes.

4. Finely slice the radishes and add to the bowl with the remaining ingredients. Pour over the other half of the dressing, toss together and serve.

tip Use any of your favourite lettuce and salad leaves in this recipe – bright, fresh green spring flavours are all beautiful together so mix and match.

ENOUGH LEFT OVER FOR:
SALAD FRY-UP (PAGE 46)
GREEN DIP (PAGE 48) ⇥⟶

Another slightly bizarre idea came about when trying to think what on earth one can do with leftover salad apart from feed it to the chickens or add it to your compost. I started to think about what would happen if you add heat – a bit like braised lettuce and peas – and it turns out it's something wonderful.

SERVES **4**
5 MINUTES TO MAKE
15 MINUTES TO COOK

SALAD FRY-UP

1 TABLESPOON OLIVE OIL

100G (3½OZ) BACON, CHORIZO, SALAMI, PARMA HAM, LEFTOVER ROAST MEAT OR SAUSAGES, CHOPPED

2 SLICES OF BREAD, CUT INTO LITTLE CUBES (STALE IS BEST)

300G (10½OZ) LEFTOVER SPRING VEGETABLE + RICOTTA SALAD (PAGE 45)

PARMESAN SHAVINGS, TO SERVE

1. Heat the oil in a frying pan or wok and fry the bacon or other meaty bits for 5–6 minutes until crispy. Add the bread cubes and gently fry for 6–8 minutes until golden and crispy, then add the salad and toss together until the leaves wilt and everything is warm. Serve with Parmesan shavings.

tip If you haven't made the Spring Vegetable + Ricotta Salad (page 45), you can just add a mixture of different leaves, peas and beans to your pan when you are frying up. Add a little drizzle of vinegar for a nice tang.

I'm a complete sucker for crisps, breadsticks, fingers of toast, anything that you can dunk into a rich, flavourful bowl of homemade dip. I always find that when you open the fridge, you can pretty much always rustle up a dip. This one uses up the bits and pieces that would ordinarily be thrown away.

SERVES **4**
15 MINUTES TO MAKE

GREEN DIP

200G (7OZ) LEFTOVER SPRING
  VEGETABLE + RICOTTA SALAD
  (PAGE 45), ESPECIALLY PEAS, BEANS,
  ASPARAGUS
1 GARLIC CLOVE, CRUSHED
A COUPLE OF DOLLOPS OF GREEK
  YOGURT, CRÈME FRAÎCHE, SOURED
  CREAM OR CREAM CHEESE OR A MIX
  OF ANY
PARMESAN, GRATED
EXTRA VIRGIN OLIVE OIL, TO DRIZZLE
SEA SALT AND FRESHLY GROUND BLACK
  PEPPER
BREADSTICKS OR TORTILLA CHIPS,
  TO SERVE

1. Whizz the leftover salad and garlic in a small food processor, add enough yogurt to loosen and form a thick paste. Add Parmesan to taste and a good drizzle of extra virgin olive oil. If it is too thick, loosen with a little cold water. Check the seasoning and serve with breadsticks or tortilla chips.

tip If you don't have any leftover Spring Vegetable + Ricotta Salad (page 45), cook 150g (5½oz) podded peas or beans, asparagus or other spring veg, then cool under cold running water. Toss with a few leaves and a little lemon juice and Dijon mustard and whizz with the remaining ingredients.

The autumn brings wonderful displays of beautiful pumpkins and squash with their firm flesh and edible skins. This is a vibrant and delicious dish either as a side or a main meal.

BAKED SQUASH WITH CHILLI + ROSEMARY

SERVES **4**, PLUS LEFTOVERS
10 MINUTES TO MAKE
45 MINUTES TO COOK

2KG (4LB 8OZ) SQUASH OR PUMPKIN,
   DESEEDED AND CUT INTO WEDGES
1 BULB GARLIC, CLOVES SEPARATED
2 RED CHILLIES, FINELY SLICED
4 SPRIGS OF ROSEMARY
OLIVE OIL, TO DRIZZLE
1 TABLESPOON CIDER VINEGAR
SEA SALT AND FRESHLY GROUND BLACK
   PEPPER
SEVERAL HANDFULS OF BABY LEAVES,
   TO SERVE

1. Preheat the oven to 200°C/fan 180°C/400°F/gas 6. Tumble the squash, garlic, chillies and rosemary into a roasting tin. Drizzle with plenty of olive oil and add the vinegar. Season with lots of sea salt and black pepper and roast for 40–45 minutes until tender. Remove the rosemary stalks, toss with the baby leaves and serve.

ENOUGH LEFT OVER FOR:
SQUASH + PARMESAN SOUFFLÉ (PAGE 52)
SQUASH LASAGNE (PAGE 53) ⇢⟶

Soufflés, they cast fear into the hearts of many cooks, but in reality they are much more robust and simple to make than you would imagine. In the past I have even removed a soufflé from the oven, dug into the centre, realized it is not quite cooked and stuck it back in to finish.

50G (1¾OZ) UNSALTED BUTTER, PLUS
    EXTRA FOR GREASING
A HANDFUL OF FRESH OR DRIED
    BREADCRUMBS, POLENTA OR
    SEMOLINA
40G (1½OZ) PLAIN FLOUR
300ML (10FL OZ) WHOLE MILK
SEA SALT AND FRESHLY GROUND BLACK
    PEPPER
4 FREE-RANGE EGGS, SEPARATED
200-250G (7-9OZ) LEFTOVER BAKED
    SQUASH WITH CHILLI + ROSEMARY
    (PAGE 49), MASHED WITH A FORK
100G (3½OZ) PARMESAN OR ANY
    OTHER CHEESE, GRATED

SQUASH + PARMESAN SOUFFLÉ

1. Preheat the oven to 200°C/fan 180°C/400°F/gas 6 and grease a deep 20cm (8in) soufflé dish with butter and then coat with a thin layer of breadcrumbs, polenta or semolina to help the mixture climb up the sides of the dish.

2. Melt the butter in a saucepan, then add the flour and cook for a couple of minutes. Add the milk, a little at a time, stirring to create a smooth sauce. Season and bubble for a minute or two.

3. Remove from the heat and stir in the egg yolks, mashed squash and Parmesan. Whisk the egg whites in a clean bowl until holding stiff peaks. Mix a dollop into the béchamel sauce, then gently fold in the remaining egg whites. Fill the soufflé dish to just below the top.

4. Place on a baking sheet and bake for 25-30 minutes until well risen and golden.

tip Without leftover Baked Squash with Chilli + Rosemary (page 49), quickly peel and deseed 250g (9oz) squash or pumpkin and steam for 10-15 minutes until softened. Mash. Heat a pan with a little olive oil and fry ½ a finely chopped red chilli and 1 finely sliced garlic clove, then mix through the mashed squash. Cool and use in the soufflé.

The rich tang of goat's cheese is completely delicious with squash, you won't miss the ragù in this gorgeous quick veggie lasagne.

SERVES **4**
20 MINUTES TO MAKE
35 MINUTES TO COOK

SQUASH LASAGNE

30G (1OZ) UNSALTED BUTTER

30G (1OZ) PLAIN FLOUR

350ML (12FL OZ) WHOLE MILK

SEA SALT AND FRESHLY GROUND BLACK
  PEPPER

6 FRESH LASAGNE SHEETS OR ANY
  PASTA, BLANCHED

300-400G (10½-14OZ) LEFTOVER BAKED
  SQUASH WITH CHILLI + ROSEMARY
  (PAGE 49), ROUGHLY CHOPPED

150G (5½OZ) GREENS OR SPINACH,
  SHREDDED AND WILTED

60G (2¼OZ) HARD GOAT'S CHEESE,
  CHEDDAR OR BLUE CHEESE,
  PARMESAN OR A MIX, GRATED

1. Preheat the oven to 200°C/fan 180°C/400°F/gas 6. Melt the butter in a pan, then add the flour and cook over a medium heat for a minute or two. Add the milk gradually, stirring constantly, until you have a thick, glossy sauce. Season well.

2. Put a little of the béchamel into the bottom of a 1.2–1.5-litre (2–2¾-pint) ovenproof dish, top with two lasagne sheets, then half the squash and blanched greens, then repeat, ending with the remaining lasagne sheets and a layer of the béchamel. Scatter over the cheese and bake for 25–30 minutes until golden.

tip If you have no leftover Baked Squash with Chilli + Rosemary (page 49), while you make the sauce, roast 400g (14oz) diced squash tossed in olive oil with a little chopped chilli and garlic until softened and then use this in the recipe.

BAKED SALMON WITH FENNEL + LEMON
FISHCAKES
SALMON + KALE OMELETTE

HERB-CRUSTED BAKED COD
SUMMER SOUP
HERBY COD GRATINÉ

GIN + HERB-CURED SALMON
CURED SALMON KEDGEREE
PINK + GREEN TART

PAN-FRIED MACKEREL WITH CAPERS + BROWN BUTTER
MACKEREL, CHIVE, LEEK + CRÈME FRAÎCHE POTS
MACKEREL + ROCKET TAGLIATELLE

ROAST COD WITH HARISSA CHICKPEAS + CAULIFLOWER
CRISPY COD PATTIES
TABBOULEH SALAD

DRESSED CRAB
FRIED CRAB BITES
CRAB PASTA

GARLIC + TOMATO PRAWNS
PRAWN COCKTAIL
PRAWN BISQUE

FISH

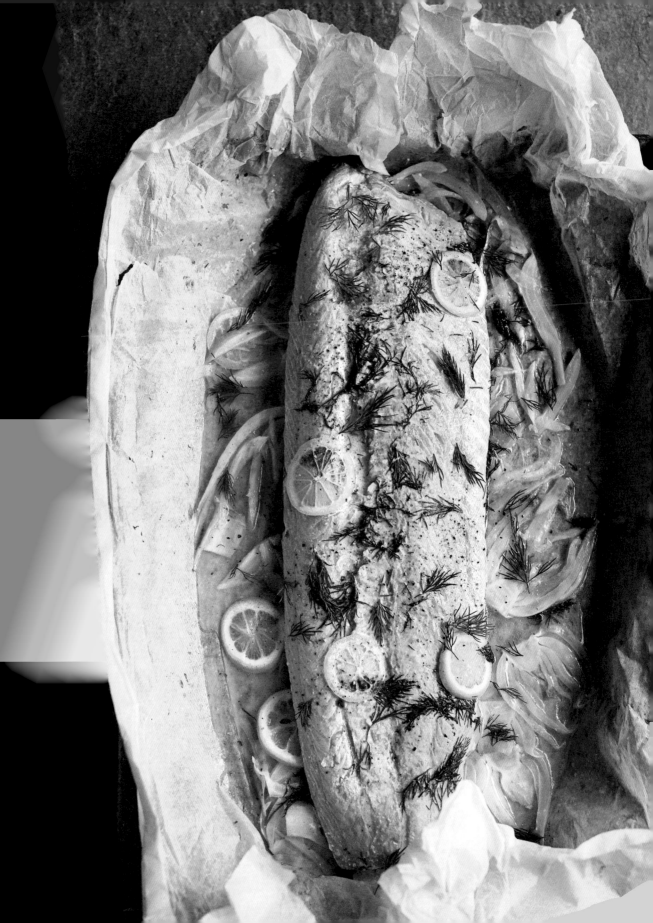

Cooking a whole fish or a large side is a wonderful way to both impress your friends and family and to ensure you have plenty of leftovers for the next day. In season, sea trout is a wonderful alternative to the usual salmon.

BAKED SALMON WITH FENNEL + LEMON

SERVES 4-6, PLUS LEFTOVERS
10 MINUTES TO MAKE
25 MINUTES TO COOK

2 BULBS FENNEL, FINELY SLICED
2 LEMONS
1 SIDE SALMON, WEIGHING
   ABOUT 750G (1LB 10OZ)
SEA SALT AND FRESHLY GROUND BLACK
   PEPPER
1 SMALL BUNCH OF DILL
GOOD KNOB OF UNSALTED BUTTER
150ML (5FL OZ) WHITE WINE OR
   VERMOUTH

1. Preheat the oven to 180°C/fan 160°C/350°F/gas 4. Line a roasting tin with foil and scatter the fennel into it. Slice one of the lemons and scatter the slices into the tin, then put the fish, skin-side down, on top. Season and scatter with the dill. Dot all over with the butter.

2. Pour the wine around the outside of the fish and add the juice of the other lemon. Bring the foil up and over and scrunch to form a parcel. Roast for 20-25 minutes until it is just opaque and you can flake it gently with a fork or the tip of a knife.

ENOUGH LEFT OVER FOR:
FISHCAKES (PAGE 58)
SALMON + KALE OMELETTE (PAGE 60) ⟫——→

There are two types of fishcakes, classic potato ones and the more adventurous Thai-style ones. I had a hard time deciding between them, but in the end the classic fishcake won. The key to a really good fishcake is the potato, it needs to be really dry and fluffy or your fishcake will become heavy and soggy.

SERVES **4**

25 MINUTES TO MAKE, PLUS
  CHILLING

45 MINUTES TO COOK

750G (1LB 10OZ) MEDIUM FLOURY
  POTATOES, SUCH AS KING EDWARD
  OR MARIS PIPER, LEFT WHOLE AND
  UNPEELED

GOOD KNOB OF UNSALTED BUTTER

SPLASH OF WHOLE MILK

300G (10½OZ) LEFTOVER BAKED
  SALMON WITH FENNEL + LEMON
  (PAGE 57)

A HANDFUL OF CHOPPED SOFT HERBS,
  SUCH AS PARSLEY, TARRAGON, DILL
  OR CHIVES

2 TABLESPOONS CHOPPED
  CORNICHONS, GHERKINS, CAPERS OR
  CAPERBERRIES

SEA SALT AND FRESHLY GROUND BLACK
  PEPPER

PLAIN FLOUR, TO DUST

2 FREE-RANGE EGGS, BEATEN

100G (3½OZ) FRESH OR DRIED
  BREADCRUMBS

SUNFLOWER OIL, TO FRY

FISHCAKES

1. Put the potatoes into a pan of cold, salted water, bring to the boil and cook for 30–45 minutes or until they are tender when pierced. Drain and leave until cold enough to handle.

2. Peel off the skins and mash or rice the potatoes and mix with the butter and milk. Stir in the fish, herbs and pickles, season and shape into eight patties. Chill for 30 minutes.

3. Dust the patties with plain flour, then dip in the beaten egg and then the breadcrumbs to coat. Heat a good layer of oil in a non-stick frying pan over a medium-high heat and fry for 5 minutes then turn over and fry until golden on both sides and hot in the centre.

tip Use flaked hot-smoked salmon or pan-fry a small piece of salmon or other fish to use in this recipe, if you haven't cooked the Baked Salmon with Fennel + Lemon on page 57.

Kale is the darling of the vegetable world at the moment, and for good reason, as it is, apart from being packed with good-for-you vitamins, really delicious. Salmon is a robust fish and is a great match for this iron-rich brassica.

150G (5½OZ) CURLY KALE OR CAVOLO
   NERO

6 FREE-RANGE EGGS

SEA SALT AND FRESHLY GROUND BLACK
   PEPPER

300G (10½OZ) LEFTOVER BAKED
   SALMON WITH FENNEL + LEMON
   (PAGE 57)

A HANDFUL OF CHOPPED SOFT
   HERBS, SUCH AS BASIL, DILL,
   PARSLEY, TARRAGON

DRIZZLE OF OLIVE OIL

FEW DOLLOPS OF CREAM CHEESE
   OR A LITTLE GRATED PARMESAN
   OR BOTH

SALMON + KALE OMELETTE

1. Plunge the kale or cavolo nero into boiling water and cook for 2–3 minutes. Drain and cool under cold running water, then finely chop.

2. Beat the eggs in a bowl with plenty of seasoning. Add the salmon, herbs and kale or cavolo nero. Mix well.

3. Heat a non-stick frying pan with a little oil over a medium-high heat and when hot, pour in half the egg mixture. Cook, stirring a little, for 2–3 minutes until almost set, add a dollop or two of cream cheese and/or a scatter of Parmesan, then fold in half and slide on to a plate. Repeat with the other half of the egg mixture and serve.

tip Use flaked hot-smoked salmon if you don't have any leftover Baked Salmon (page 57).

Pressing a crust on to fish before baking is a great way to add loads of extra flavour and texture to the finished dish. It also protects the delicate fish from the heat of the oven so that the fish cooks perfectly.

HERB-CRUSTED BAKED COD

SERVES **4**, PLUS LEFTOVERS
15 MINUTES TO MAKE
15 MINUTES TO COOK

2 SIDES OF COD FILLET, WEIGHING
   ABOUT 350G (12OZ) EACH
SEA SALT AND FRESHLY GROUND BLACK
   PEPPER
150G (5½OZ) FRESH WHITE
   BREADCRUMBS
1 GARLIC CLOVE, CRUSHED
ZEST OF 1 LEMON
A HANDFUL OF CHOPPED FLAT-LEAF
   PARSLEY
A HANDFUL OF CHOPPED SOFT HERBS,
   SUCH AS TARRAGON, CHIVES OR DILL
2 TABLESPOONS MAYONNAISE
1 TABLESPOON DIJON MUSTARD
2 TABLESPOONS CAPERS, CHOPPED
EXTRA VIRGIN OLIVE OIL, TO DRIZZLE

1. Preheat the oven to 200°C/fan 180°C/400°F/gas 6 and line a baking tray with nonstick baking paper.

2. Season the fish all over with salt and pepper and put on the lined tray. Mix the remaining ingredients together, adding enough olive oil to bind and season. Press the mixture all over the fish and bake in the top of the oven for 12–15 minutes until the fish is just cooked and the crust is golden.

ENOUGH LEFT OVER FOR:
SUMMER SOUP (PAGE 64)
HERB COD GRATINÉ (PAGE 64) »——→

An English summer is full to bursting with amazing green tender vegetables and what better way to celebrate them than in the most simple broth with flakes of white fish and crispy crumbs.

• • •   • • • • • • •   •   •   •   • • •   •   • • •   • • • • • •   •   •   •   • • • •   •   • • •   •   • • •   •   •

SERVES **4** AS A STARTER
10 MINUTES TO MAKE
20 MINUTES TO COOK

SUMMER SOUP

1 TABLESPOON OLIVE OIL

1 LARGE ONION, FINELY SLICED

2 GARLIC CLOVES, CRUSHED

400G (14OZ) GREEN SUMMER
  VEGETABLES, SUCH AS LEEKS, PEAS,
  OR ASPARAGUS, SLICED IF NECESSARY

150ML (5FL OZ) WHITE WINE

500ML (18FL OZ) VEGETABLE STOCK

SEA SALT AND FRESHLY GROUND BLACK
  PEPPER

300G (10½OZ) LEFTOVER HERB-CRUSTED
  BAKED COD (PAGE 63)

1. Heat the oil in a pan and fry the onion for 10 minutes until softened. Add the garlic and the green vegetables and stir well for 30 seconds. Add the wine and bubble for a couple of minutes, then add the stock. Season and simmer for 5–10 minutes.

2. Flake the fish, keeping the crust aside, and add to the soup. Once hot, serve in deep bowls with a scattering of the crust over the top.

Here a simple white sauce and cheesy crust transforms leftover fish into a supper to chase away the rainy day blues.

• • •   • • • • • • •   •   •   •   • • •   •   • • •   • • • • • •   •   •   •   • • • •   •   • • •   •   • • •   •   •

SERVES **2**
15 MINUTES TO MAKE
15 MINUTES TO COOK

HERBY COD GRATINÉ

20G (¾OZ) UNSALTED BUTTER

20G (¾OZ) PLAIN FLOUR

250ML (9FL OZ) WHOLE MILK

2 TEASPOONS DIJON MUSTARD

SEA SALT AND FRESHLY GROUND BLACK
  PEPPER

300G (10½OZ) GREEN VEGETABLES,
  SUCH AS LEEKS, PEAS, SPROUTS

200G (7OZ) LEFTOVER HERB-CRUSTED
  BAKED COD (PAGE 63)

A HANDFUL OF SOFT HERBS, SUCH AS
  TARRAGON, PARSLEY, CHIVES OR DILL

25G (1OZ) GRATED CHEESE, SUCH AS
  CHEDDAR, GRUYÈRE OR PARMESAN

1. Preheat the oven to 200°C/fan 180°C/400°F/gas 6. Melt the butter in a pan, add the flour and cook for 2–3 minutes, then gradually add the milk, stirring until you have a thick, creamy sauce. Add the mustard and season well.

2. Blanch the green vegetables and add to the white sauce. Remove the crust from the fish and set aside. Flake the fish into the sauce, chop the herbs and add them too and stir together.

3. Spoon into an ovenproof dish. Break the crust up into small pieces and scatter over the top along with the cheese. Bake for 10–12 minutes until bubbling and hot.

tip If you don't have the leftover cod (page 63), simply pan-fry 300g (10½oz) cod or white fish fillet until just cooked. Flake and mix with the white sauce. Scatter over a handful of breadcrumbs.

Why is it that curing your own salmon seems to be something only ever done for big celebrations such as Christmas or Easter? It makes for a fantastic supper standby as well as being on hand for breakfasts, lunches and canapés.

GIN + HERB-CURED SALMON

SERVES 4-6, PLUS LEFTOVERS
20 MINUTES TO MAKE
3-4 DAYS TO CURE

1.5KG (3LB 5OZ) WHOLE SALMON, FILLETED, SKIN ON
100ML (3½FL OZ) GIN
75G (2¾OZ) DEMERARA SUGAR
50G (1¾OZ) SEA SALT
GOOD GRINDING OF BLACK PEPPER
25G (1OZ) DILL, FINELY CHOPPED
2 TABLESPOONS JUNIPER BERRIES
SLICES OF WHITE OR BROWN BREAD, SOFTENED UNSALTED BUTTER AND LEMON WEDGES, TO SERVE

1. Remove any bones from the salmon. Place one half, skin-side down, on a large piece of foil topped with a large piece of clingfilm. Rub with half the gin, then mix the sugar, salt, pepper, herbs and juniper berries together and press over the salmon fillet.

2. Drizzle with a little more gin, then place the other fillet, skin-side up, on top. Sprinkle with the remaining gin, then fold the clingfilm up and over and tightly seal the salmon. Then bring the foil up and tightly seal that around the fish.

3. Place on a wire rack in a roasting tin or on a platter and then put a chopping board on top and weigh it down with some cans. Put the whole lot in the fridge and leave for 3-4 days, turning from time to time.

4. When ready, remove the wrappings and gently scrape away the salty herb mix with your finger and wipe with damp kitchen paper. Use a very sharp knife to cut thin slices of salmon away from the skin. Butter the slices of white or brown bread and serve with the cured salmon and lemon wedges. The salmon will keep in the fridge for at least a week.

ENOUGH LEFT OVER FOR:
CURED SALMON KEDGEREE (PAGE 68)
PINK + GREEN TART (PAGE 70) »——→

My mother used to make kedgeree for us all the time, both the classic smoked haddock version and a cheat's version with canned tuna, which is one of my store cupboard suppers to this day. So the idea of using cured salmon in kedgeree was just the next step in the journey and it turns out it is gloriously delicious!

SERVES **4**
10 MINUTES TO MAKE
15 MINUTES TO COOK

3 FREE-RANGE EGGS

1 TABLESPOON OLIVE OIL

GOOD KNOB OF UNSALTED BUTTER

1 LARGE ONION, FINELY SLICED

1 TEASPOON GROUND TURMERIC

350G (12OZ) BASMATI RICE

300G (10½OZ) LEFTOVER GIN + HERB-
   CURED SALMON (PAGE 67), SLICED

GOOD GLUG OF DOUBLE CREAM

A HANDFUL OF FLAT-LEAF PARSLEY,
   CHOPPED

SEA SALT AND FRESHLY GROUND BLACK
   PEPPER

CURED SALMON KEDGEREE

1. Put the eggs into a pan of cold water, bring to the boil and boil for 6 minutes. Drain and cool in cold water.

2. Meanwhile, heat the oil and butter in a pan and fry the onion for 10 minutes. Add the turmeric and stir for a minute.

3. In the meantime, rinse the rice and then cook in a saucepan of boiling, salted water for 10–12 minutes until tender. Drain and add to the onion pan and toss to coat in the buttery yellowness. Add the salmon, cream and parsley and season well. Peel and halve the eggs and serve on top of scoops of the kedgeree.

tip If you don't have the Gin + Herb-cured Salmon (page 67), you can use smoked salmon instead or try flaked hot-smoked salmon or even good-quality canned tuna.

Pink for salmon, green for whatever greeny veg you might have in your fridge, it really is that simple. I love making my own pastry, and find that I always have the ingredients to hand, but a ready-rolled shortcrust would work well here too.

SERVES **4**

30 MINUTES TO MAKE, PLUS CHILLING

50 MINUTES TO COOK

PINK + GREEN TART

FOR THE PASTRY

200G (7OZ) PLAIN FLOUR, PLUS EXTRA TO DUST

PINCH OF SEA SALT

150G (5½OZ) CHILLED UNSALTED BUTTER, CUBED

FOR THE FILLING

1 TABLESPOON OLIVE OIL

1 BUNCH OF SPRING ONIONS, FINELY SLICED

200G (7OZ) LEFTOVER GIN + HERB-CURED SALMON (PAGE 67), SLICED

200G (7OZ) GREEN VEGETABLES, SUCH AS ASPARAGUS, GREENS, SPROUTING BROCCOLI, SLICED AND BLANCHED IF NECESSARY

300ML (10FL OZ) DOUBLE CREAM, CRÈME FRAÎCHE OR A MIX OF BOTH

2 FREE-RANGE EGGS, PLUS 1 FREE-RANGE YOLK

2 TEASPOONS DIJON MUSTARD

A HANDFUL OF CHOPPED SOFT HERBS, SUCH AS TARRAGON, DILL OR PARSLEY

SEA SALT AND FRESHLY GROUND BLACK PEPPER

1. To make the pastry, blend the flour and salt together in a bowl, then rub the cubes of butter in with your fingers until the mixture resembles breadcrumbs. Add 1–2 tablespoons of cold water and bring the mixture together with the flat of a knife, then with your hands. Knead briefly and shape into a disc. Wrap in clingfilm and chill for 15 minutes.

2. Meanwhile, for the filling, heat the oil in a saucepan and fry the spring onions for 5 minutes until softened. Tip into a bowl and add the salmon and green vegetables.

3. In a jug, whisk the cream or crème fraîche with the eggs, yolk, mustard and herbs. Season.

4. Roll out the pastry on a lightly floured surface to 2mm (⅛in) in thickness and use to line a 20–23cm (8–9in) square or round tart tin. Chill for 10 minutes.

5. Preheat the oven to 200°C/fan 180°C/400°F/gas 6. Line the tart case with foil or nonstick baking paper and baking beans or uncooked rice. Blind bake for 12–15 minutes, then remove the foil/paper and beans/rice and return to the oven for a further 5 minutes.

6. Scatter the tart with the salmon mixture and pour over the egg and cream mixture. Reduce the oven temperature to 160°C/fan 140°C/350°F/gas 3 and bake for 20–30 minutes until just set. Leave to cool for at least 10 minutes before serving warm or at room temperature.

tip Use thin slices of smoked salmon if you don't have the cured salmon leftovers from page 67.

Mackerel is at its best when it's spankingly fresh so, if you can, get yours from a good fishmonger and ask them to butterfly them for you. The capers cut through the oily flavour of the fish. Serve this simply with crusty bread or boiled new potatoes.

PAN-FRIED MACKEREL WITH CAPERS + BROWN BUTTER

SERVES **4**, PLUS LEFTOVERS
5 MINUTES TO MAKE
10 MINUTES TO COOK

1 TABLESPOON OLIVE OIL

6 MACKEREL, BUTTERFLIED

80G (2¾OZ) UNSALTED BUTTER

ZEST AND JUICE OF 1 LEMON

3 TABLESPOONS SMALL CAPERS,
    DRAINED AND RINSED

A HANDFUL OF FLAT-LEAF PARSLEY,
    FINELY CHOPPED

CRUSTY BREAD OR BOILED NEW
    POTATOES, TO SERVE

1. Heat a layer of oil in a non-stick frying pan and fry the mackerel, skin-side down, one or two at a time, for 4–5 minutes until golden brown, then flip over and cook for 1 minute until just cooked through. Remove from the pan and keep warm in a low oven (about 110°C/fan 90°C/225°F/gas ½) while you cook the remaining fish, adding each to the oven to keep warm once cooked.

2. Add the butter to the pan and allow it to foam and start to become brown and nutty. Stir in the lemon zest and juice, capers and parsley. Serve the mackerel with the capers and butter and crusty bread or boiled new potatoes.

tip It takes no extra time to cook two more mackerel and you will reap the rewards the next day.

ENOUGH LEFT OVER FOR:
MACKEREL, CHIVE, LEEK + CRÈME FRAÎCHE POTS
    (PAGE 74)
MACKEREL + ROCKET TAGLIATELLE (PAGE 74) »——→

A great little starter or a perfect nibble to serve with
a glass of bubbles.

SERVES **4-6**
5 MINUTES TO MAKE
5 MINUTES TO COOK

MACKEREL, CHIVE, LEEK + CRÈME FRAÎCHE POTS

GOOD KNOB OF UNSALTED BUTTER
2 LEEKS, FINELY SLICED
200G (7OZ) LEFTOVER PAN-FRIED
   MACKEREL WITH CAPERS + BROWN
   BUTTER (PAGE 73), FLAKED
1 BUNCH OF CHIVES, SNIPPED
150G (5½OZ) CRÈME FRAÎCHE
1 LEMON, ZEST AND SQUEEZE OF JUICE
2 TEASPOONS CREAMED HORSERADISH
SEA SALT AND FRESHLY GROUND BLACK
   PEPPER
FINGERS OF TOAST, TO SERVE

1. Heat the butter in a saucepan and gently fry the leeks for
5–6 minutes until soft. Tip into a bowl and set aside to cool.
Once cooled, mix with the remaining ingredients. Season and
spoon into small ramekins or pots and serve with toast fingers.

tip If you don't have leftover mackerel from page 73, use 200g
(7oz) hot-smoked mackerel and add 2 teaspoons of drained and
rinsed capers instead.

Pasta is probably most people's go-to store cupboard supper and
a little leftover mackerel is just the thing to toss through at the end.
Many Italians say never to serve Parmesan with fish, but with pasta
I always find it really rather good.

SERVES **4**
5 MINUTES TO MAKE
12 MINUTES TO COOK

MACKEREL + ROCKET TAGLIATELLE

350G (12OZ) TAGLIATELLE OR OTHER
   LONG PASTA
200G (7OZ) LEFTOVER PAN-FRIED
   MACKEREL WITH CAPERS + BROWN
   BUTTER (PAGE 73), FLAKED
GOOD KNOB OF UNSALTED BUTTER
SPLASH OF CREAM, CRÈME FRAÎCHE
   OR SOURED CREAM
100G (3½OZ) ROCKET
FRESHLY GROUND BLACK PEPPER
PARMESAN SHAVINGS, TO SERVE

1. Cook the pasta in boiling, salted water according to the packet
instructions or until just cooked. Drain and return to the pan
with a splash of cooking liquid and add the mackerel, butter,
cream and rocket. Season with plenty of black pepper and serve
scattered with Parmesan shavings.

tip Use 200g (7oz) flaked hot-smoked mackerel if you haven't
cooked the Pan-fried Mackerel with Capers + Brown Butter
(page 73).

Roasting cauliflower makes such a difference, instead of absorbing all the water from steaming, it soaks up flavour like a sponge. Any firm, meaty white fish would be great in this recipe, something like haddock or even monkfish is fantastic.

ROAST COD WITH HARISSA CHICKPEAS + CAULIFLOWER

SERVES 4, PLUS LEFTOVERS
5 MINUTES TO MAKE
45 MINUTES TO COOK

1 CAULIFLOWER, BROKEN INTO
  FLORETS
2 TABLESPOONS OLIVE OIL
2 TABLESPOONS ROSE HARISSA
400G (14OZ) CAN OF CHOPPED
  TOMATOES
SPLASH OF VEGETABLE STOCK OR
  WATER
400G (14OZ) CAN OF CHICKPEAS,
  DRAINED AND RINSED
800G (1LB 12OZ) CHUNKY COD FILLETS
1 TABLESPOON OLIVE OIL
FRESH CORIANDER, CHOPPED,
  TO SCATTER

1. Preheat the oven to 190°C/fan 170°C/375°F/gas 5. Put the cauliflower into a roasting tin and toss with the oil and harissa. Roast for 25–30 minutes, turning occasionally.

2. Stir in the tomatoes and stock or water. Mix in the chickpeas, then place the cod on top, drizzle with the oil and season. Roast for a further 10–12 minutes until the cod is just cooked. Scatter with coriander and serve.

ENOUGH LEFT OVER FOR:
CRISPY COD PATTIES (PAGE 77)
TABBOULEH SALAD (PAGE 77) »⟶

I can't resist a patty, if I read the word on a menu I am instantly hooked. Little fried delicate patties of deliciousness. These guys are a little fragile so let them fry for a good few minutes over a medium heat until they have a nice crust before you flip them.

MAKES **8**
10 MINUTES TO MAKE, PLUS
   CHILLING
10 MINUTES TO COOK

CRISPY COD PATTIES

300G (10½OZ) LEFTOVER ROAST COD
   WITH HARISSA CHICKPEAS +
   CAULIFLOWER (PAGE 76)
400G (14OZ) CAN OF CHICKPEAS,
   DRAINED AND RINSED
2 BEETROOT, PEELED AND GRATED
1 FREE-RANGE EGG, BEATEN
ZEST AND JUICE OF 1 LEMON
SEA SALT AND FRESHLY GROUND
   BLACK PEPPER
SUNFLOWER OIL, TO FRY
PLAIN FLOUR, TO DUST
GREEK OR NATURAL YOGURT, TO SERVE

1. Mash up the leftover cod, chickpeas and cauliflower and the additional can of chickpeas with a fork to form a rough paste. Add the grated beetroot, egg, lemon zest and juice and season to taste. Shape into eight patties and chill for 30 minutes.

2. Heat a good layer of oil in a non-stick frying pan. Dust the patties in flour and fry over a medium heat for 3–4 minutes on each side until golden. Serve with yogurt.

The thing about tabbouleh is that it is more about the parsley than about the bulgur wheat, so don't be shy when adding it to the bowl.

SERVES **4** AS A LUNCH OR **6** AS A SIDE
10 MINUTES TO MAKE
15 MINUTES TO COOK

TABBOULEH SALAD

300G (10½OZ) BULGUR WHEAT
550ML (19FL OZ) VEGETABLE STOCK OR
   WATER
1 CUCUMBER OR COURGETTE
A HANDFUL OF ROUGHLY CHOPPED
   SOFT HERBS, SUCH AS TARRAGON,
   DILL OR PARSLEY
ZEST AND JUICE OF 1 LEMON
A GLUG OF EXTRA VIRGIN OLIVE OIL
300G (10½OZ) LEFTOVER ROAST COD
   WITH HARISSA CHICKPEAS +
   CAULIFLOWER (PAGE 76)
SEA SALT AND FRESHLY GROUND
   BLACK PEPPER

1. Put the bulgur wheat in a saucepan and cover with the stock or water. Bring to the boil, then cover and set aside, off the heat, for 15 minutes until the liquid has been absorbed.

2. Use a peeler to peel the cucumber or courgette into ribbons. Toss them with the bulgur wheat and the remaining ingredients. Season and serve.

tip If you don't have leftovers from the Roast Cod with Harissa Chickpeas + Cauliflower (page 76), break 150g (5½oz) raw cauliflower into small florets or whizz into crumbs. Mix with a 400g (14oz) can of chickpeas, drained and rinsed. Pan-fry a 150g (5½oz) cod fillet and flake up to toss through the salad at the end. Add a little dollop of rose harissa to the stock before pouring over the bulgur wheat.

A perfectly dressed crab is a thing of beauty. It is simple these days to buy them from good fishmongers, but for me, the process of cracking open a just-cooked crab, with all its sea-fresh juices, and picking out the hard-to-get white meat, somehow makes the end result all the sweeter. A prize for all the hard work.

SERVES **4**, PLUS LEFTOVERS
1 HOUR TO MAKE, PLUS FREEZING
15 MINUTES TO COOK

DRESSED CRAB

4 LIVE LARGE BROWN CRABS,
   WEIGHING ABOUT 900G–1KG
   (2LB–2LB 4OZ) EACH
25G (1OZ) FRESH WHITE BREADCRUMBS
FEW DASHES OF TABASCO SAUCE
GOOD SQUEEZE OF LEMON JUICE
2–3 TABLESPOONS MAYONNAISE
PINCH OF GROUND MACE
HOT TOAST, TO SERVE

1. Put the crabs in the freezer for 15 minutes. Bring a very large pan of water to the boil and drop in the crabs. Cover and boil for 15 minutes. Remove from the water and set aside to cool.

2. Twist the claws and legs off the bodies and set aside for now. Put each crab on its back. Hold the edges of the shell with your fingers and then use your thumbs to push on where the leg section joins the body and lever the body away from the leg.

3. Pull off the feathery soft dead man's fingers sticking out from the body. Scoop out the bony, gloopy bits from behind the eyes and discard.

4. Scrape out all the brown meat from the sides of the shell into a bowl and set aside. Use the back of a heavy knife or hammer to crack open the claws so that you can remove all of the juicy meat. Make sure you break open the knuckles and legs to get every last bit.

tips Choose crabs that feel heavy for their size. If your pan isn't very large, cook the crabs one or two at a time. Make sure the water comes fully to the boil before adding the next crab.

5. Cut the body section in half and use a skewer or lobster pick to pick out all the sweet white meat from the many compartments. Wash and dry the shells.

6. Mix the brown crabmeat with the breadcrumbs and Tabasco and spoon into the sides of each shell. Mix the white meat with the lemon juice, mayonnaise and mace and spoon into the centre of the shells. Serve with hot toast.

ENOUGH LEFT OVER FOR:
FRIED CRAB BITES (PAGE 80)
CRAB PASTA (PAGE 82) ⟫⟶

Naughty but nice, these golden fried nuggets of crab are really moreish with a little squidge of lemon. They brown in seconds in the oil so watch them like a hawk in case they go too dark.

FRIED CRAB BITES

175G (6OZ) LEFTOVER DRESSED CRAB
  (PAGE 79)
100G (3½OZ) RITZ BISCUITS, WATER
  BISCUITS OR SIMPLE CRACKERS,
  CRUSHED TO CRUMBS
FEW DROPS OF TABASCO SAUCE
2 TEASPOONS DIJON MUSTARD
SUNFLOWER OIL, FOR DEEP-FRYING
1 FREE-RANGE EGG, BEATEN
LEMON WEDGES, TO SERVE

1. Mix the crab with 2 teaspoons of the crushed crackers and the Tabasco and mustard. Shape into 8–10 walnut-sized balls and chill for 20 minutes.

2. Heat the oil in a small but deep pan until it reaches 180°C/350°F or a cube of bread browns in 30 seconds.

3. Dip each ball in the beaten egg and then into the remaining crushed crackers and deep-fry for a minute or so until golden brown. Serve straight away with lemon wedges on the side.

tip Buy a medium dressed crab to make this recipe if you haven't dressed your own crab (page 79).

A freshly dressed crab is heaven but it is quite rich, so I often find I have some left over and always think simple is best when it comes to such a delicious treat. Tossed through pasta with fresh herbs is about as good as a second helping of crab gets.

SERVES **4**

5 MINUTES TO MAKE

12 MINUTES TO COOK

350G (12OZ) LINGUINE OR OTHER LONG
   PASTA

SEA SALT AND FRESHLY GROUND BLACK
   PEPPER

EXTRA VIRGIN OLIVE OIL, TO DRIZZLE

200G (7OZ) LEFTOVER DRESSED CRAB
   (PAGE 79)

A HANDFUL OF CHOPPED SOFT HERBS,
   SUCH AS PARSLEY, TARRAGON,
   CHIVES, DILL OR BASIL

GRATED PARMESAN, TO SERVE

CRAB PASTA

1. Cook the pasta in boiling, salted water according to the packet instructions until just cooked and al dente. Return to the pan with a little of the cooking water and a good drizzle of extra virgin olive oil.

2. Toss through the crab and herbs and season with sea salt and plenty of freshly ground black pepper. Serve immediately with Parmesan grated over the top.

tip Use a mix of mostly white with a little brown crabmeat if you didn't dress your own crab (page 79).

Served as a simple quick supper or as part of a tapas menu for friends, these prawns are simply delicious. A cunning little trick is to buy raw prawns in their shells, that way, even if you have very few prawns left after scoffing, you have the shells and heads to make a fabulous stock or soup.

GARLIC + TOMATO PRAWNS

SERVES **4**, PLUS LEFTOVERS
10 MINUTES TO MAKE
20 MINUTES TO COOK

2 TABLESPOONS OLIVE OIL

1 BANANA SHALLOT, FINELY CHOPPED

3 GARLIC CLOVES, FINELY SLICED

125ML (4FL OZ) DRY WHITE WINE

A SPRIG OF ROSEMARY

400G (14OZ) CAN OF CHERRY
    TOMATOES

700G (1LB 9OZ) SHELL-ON RAW KING
    PRAWNS

SEA SALT AND FRESHLY GROUND BLACK
    PEPPER

1. Heat the oil in a pan and gently fry the shallot for 5 minutes, then add the garlic and cook for 30 seconds. Add the wine, rosemary and tomatoes and bubble for 10–12 minutes, then add the prawns and cook until they are pink. Season to taste and serve immediately. Keep the heads and shells for the Prawn Bisque on page 87.

ENOUGH LEFT OVER FOR:
PRAWN COCKTAIL (PAGE 86)
PRAWN BISQUE (PAGE 87) ⟶

Now considered by many to be so retro that it is cool again, the humble prawn cocktail is always a winner. Using up the leftover Garlic + Tomato Prawns (page 83) adds a whole new dimension to the dish, which once tried you may never do any other way.

SERVES **4**
10 MINUTES TO MAKE

PRAWN COCKTAIL

150G (5½OZ) LEFTOVER GARLIC + TOMATO PRAWNS - ABOUT 8-10 PRAWNS AND 4-5 TABLESPOONS SAUCE (PAGE 83)
5 TABLESPOONS MAYONNAISE
A SQUIDGE OF TOMATO KETCHUP
DASH OF TABASCO SAUCE
DASH OF WORCESTERSHIRE SAUCE
SQUEEZE OF LEMON JUICE
TINY SPLASH OF SHERRY
SEA SALT AND FRESHLY GROUND BLACK PEPPER
ANY GREEN SALAD BITS YOU HAVE, SUCH AS LETTUCE, AVOCADO, CUCUMBER
CRUSTY BREAD OR TOAST, TO SERVE

1. Remove any prawns from the sauce, peel and roughly chop. Mix the sauce with the mayonnaise, tomato ketchup, Tabasco, Worcestershire sauce, lemon juice and sherry. Season to taste and stir in the chopped prawns.

2. Chop any salad bits you have and put on to small plates. Top with the prawn cocktail and serve with crusty bread or toast.

tip If you haven't made the Garlic + Tomato Prawns on page 83, you can make a more classic prawn cocktail. Mix 10 cooked, peeled prawns, chopped if king prawns, with the remaining ingredients, adding a little more mayo and tomato ketchup.

The word bisque makes this recipe sound way more difficult or flashy than it really is, it is just that to call it a soup would be to do it an injustice as it has such a fabulous depth of flavour and a silky smoothness from the prawn shells.

SERVES **4** AS A STARTER
15 MINUTES TO MAKE
50 MINUTES TO COOK

PRAWN BISQUE

2 TABLESPOONS OLIVE OIL

200-300G (7-10½OZ) PRAWN SHELLS (SEE PAGE 83)

1 ONION, FINELY SLICED

1 CARROT, FINELY CHOPPED

2 TEASPOONS GREEN FENNEL SEEDS

150ML (5FL OZ) WHITE WINE

100-150G (3½-5½OZ) LEFTOVER GARLIC + TOMATO PRAWNS (PAGE 83)

400G (14OZ) CAN OF CHOPPED TOMATOES

700ML (1¼ PINTS) FISH OR VEGETABLE STOCK

GOOD SPLASH OF DOUBLE CREAM, CRÈME FRAÎCHE OR SOURED CREAM, PLUS EXTRA TO SERVE

SEA SALT AND FRESHLY GROUND BLACK PEPPER

A HANDFUL OF SOFT HERBS, SUCH AS DILL, PARSLEY, TARRAGON OR FENNEL, FINELY CHOPPED, TO SERVE

1. Heat the oil in a pan and fry the shells from the prawns, the onion, carrot and fennel seeds for 10 minutes until the vegetables are lovely and soft. Add the wine and bubble for a minute.

2. Remove any leftover prawns from the sauce and set aside. Add the leftover sauce along with the canned tomatoes and stock to the pan and simmer for 30 minutes.

3. Blitz the soup as finely as you can (shells and all), then pour through a sieve into a bowl, pressing as much of the mixture through the sieve as you can.

4. Tip back into a clean pan and bring to the boil. Chop the prawns and add them to the pan with a good splash of cream, then whizz. Season to taste and serve with extra cream, crème fraiche or soured cream and any soft herbs you have knocking about.

tip Buy 300g (10½oz) shell-on prawns to use in this recipe if you haven't made the Garlic + Tomato Prawns (page 83).

GRIDDLED CHICKEN WITH KALE, TARRAGON + HAZELNUT PESTO
LINGUINE WITH KALE PESTO + CRISPY CHICKEN SKIN
CHICKEN + WHITE BEANS

CHICKEN HAINAN
SOUL SOUP
COCONUT + CHILLI CHICKEN POTS

ROAST CHICKEN WITH LEMON + TARRAGON
ROAST CHICKEN + MUSHROOM RISOTTO
QUICK CHICKEN, PURPLE SPROUTING BROCCOLI + STICKY CHILLI STIR-FRY

CHARGRILLED LAMB SHOULDER
FATTEH
LAMB KARAHI

SPICE-CRUSTED RUMP CAP WITH PUY LENTIL SALAD
TAGLIATA
BEEF WITH BÉARNAISE SAUCE + CHIPS

SLOW-COOKED BEEF RAGÙ
BEEF + BARLEY SOUP
SMOKY BEEF EMPANADAS

STICKY BRAISED SHORT RIBS
THAI BEEF SALAD
BEEF SUMMER ROLLS

SLOW-ROAST JUNIPER + FENNEL SEED PORK BELLY
GOULASH
SHREDDED PORK + APPLE BUNS

PAN-ROASTED PORK CHOPS WITH APPLES + ONIONS
SPICED PORK WITH HARISSA CHICKPEAS
RAINBOW SALAD

MEAT

Pesto is so much more than the classic basil and pine nut variety. I love experimenting with different green veg and hard cheeses to see what new deliciousness awaits. You don't have to use all kale – swap some for parsley instead, or try using Brussels sprouts! You can also use Pecorino or Manchego as an alternative to Parmesan.

GRIDDLED CHICKEN WITH KALE, TARRAGON + HAZELNUT PESTO

SERVES **4**, PLUS LEFTOVERS
15 MINUTES TO MAKE
25 MINUTES TO COOK

4 FREE-RANGE SKIN-ON CHICKEN
   BREASTS
500G (1LB 2OZ) NEW POTATOES
SEA SALT AND FRESHLY GROUND BLACK
   PEPPER
2 TABLESPOONS OLIVE OIL

FOR THE PESTO
200G (7OZ) CURLY KALE, CAVOLO NERO
   OR BRUSSELS SPROUTS
2-3 SPRIGS OF TARRAGON, LEAVES
   STRIPPED
150-200ML (5-7FL OZ) EXTRA VIRGIN
   OLIVE OIL
2 GARLIC CLOVES, CRUSHED
70G (2½OZ) HAZELNUTS, BLANCHED
100G (3½OZ) PARMESAN, GRATED
LEMON JUICE, TO TASTE

1. Remove the skin from the chicken breasts and keep for the Linguine with Kale Pesto + Crispy Chicken Skin (page 92). Put the chicken breasts between pieces of clingfilm or nonstick baking paper and bash with a rolling pin until about 1cm (½in) thick.

2. Tip the potatoes into a pan of cold salted water, bring to the boil and simmer until tender. Drain and crush with a fork, then toss with most of the olive oil and some seasoning.

3. Heat a griddle pan over a high heat. Brush the chicken with the remaining oil, season well and griddle for 2-3 minutes on each side until just cooked. Set aside to rest.

4. For the pesto, shred the kale and plunge into a pan of boiling water for a minute to just start to cook it, drain and refresh under cold water, then whizz with the remaining ingredients. Season to taste with sea salt, black pepper and lemon juice. Slice the chicken (hold back one breast for another time) and serve with the crushed potatoes and half of the pesto. Keep the remaining pesto for another recipe – it will keep in the fridge for up to a week.

tips Buy skin-on chicken breasts and remove the skin to use in leftovers recipes to add a hit of chicken flavour.

Slicing a chicken breast makes it go much further – 3 breasts will feed 4 people as a main meal, but if you buy and cook 4 chicken breasts you can save one or even 1½ to use in leftovers dishes.

ENOUGH LEFT OVER FOR:
LINGUINE WITH KALE PESTO + CRISPY CHICKEN SKIN
   (PAGE 92)
CHICKEN + WHITE BEANS (PAGE 94) ⟶

It can be hard to find chicken breasts with the skin on these days, as if we are all afraid of them, when in reality the skin is one of the tastiest bits of the bird. By saving the skins from the meal on page 91, you can get all that savoury chicken-y hit into your pasta without the need to add any meat at all!

LINGUINE WITH KALE PESTO + CRISPY CHICKEN SKIN

SERVES **4**
5 MINUTES TO MAKE
15 MINUTES TO COOK

SKIN FROM 4 FREE-RANGE CHICKEN
  BREASTS (SEE PAGE 91)
350G (12OZ) LINGUINE OR OTHER PASTA
150–200G (5½–7OZ) KALE, TARRAGON +
  HAZELNUT PESTO (PAGE 91)
GRATED PARMESAN CHEESE, TO SERVE

1. Preheat the oven to 200°C/fan 180°C/400°F/gas 6. Put the chicken skin on a lipped baking sheet and put another baking sheet on top. Roast for 10–12 minutes until the skin is crispy. Pour off the fat into a small bowl and set the skin aside.

2. Cook the pasta in a saucepan of boiling salted water for 10–12 minutes until just cooked. Drain and toss with 1 tablespoon of the chicken fat, 1 tablespoon of the cooking water and the pesto. Crush the chicken skin into crunchy pieces.

3. Divide the pasta between warmed bowls and scatter with the crispy skin and grated Parmesan.

tip If you haven't already made the pesto, make half the quantity in the recipe for Griddled Chicken with Kale, Tarragon + Hazelnut Pesto on page 91.

There is something so comforting about soft and creamy beans melting into sauces and stews. Canned beans are an absolute staple in my store cupboard and they are ideal for making leftovers suppers a doddle.

SERVES **4**
10 MINUTES TO MAKE
15 MINUTES TO COOK

1 TABLESPOON OLIVE OIL

100G (3½OZ) CHORIZO, STREAKY BACON, PANCETTA OR SALAMI, FINELY CHOPPED

1 LARGE ONION, FINELY SLICED

2 GARLIC CLOVES, CRUSHED

A FEW SPRIGS OF THYME, PLUS EXTRA TO GARNISH

400G (14OZ) CAN OF WHITE BEANS (BUTTER OR CANNELLINI ARE PERFECT), DRAINED AND RINSED

200ML (7FL OZ) CHICKEN STOCK (PAGE 101)

1–1½ LEFTOVER GRIDDLED CHICKEN BREASTS (PAGE 91), FINELY SLICED

SPLASH OF DOUBLE CREAM OR A DOLLOP OF CRÈME FRAÎCHE

JUICE OF ½ LEMON

SEA SALT AND FRESHLY GROUND BLACK PEPPER

CHICKEN + WHITE BEANS

1. Heat the oil in a pan and fry the chorizo or other meaty bits for a few minutes until crispy. Remove with a slotted spoon and set aside. Add the onion to the pan and fry for 5 minutes until softened, then add the garlic, thyme and the chorizo and stir for 30 seconds.

2. Add the beans and stock and bubble for 5 minutes then add the sliced chicken, cream or crème fraîche and lemon juice. Season to taste and serve with the extra parsley scattered over the top.

tip If you haven't cooked the Griddled Chicken with Kale, Tarragon + Hazelnut Pesto on page 91, use 1 (or 2 small) free-range chicken breasts. Slice them thinly and pan-fry them with the onion at the start of the recipe.

Until you have tried it, it's hard to explain the joy of a big steaming bowl of Hainan chicken. This is one of those dishes that puts the world to rights no matter what kind of day you are having. This is an homage to my dear friend Dhruv Baker who introduced me to this amazing dish. I've slightly simplified my version, but I don't think he will mind me saying it is just as perfectly delicious.

SERVES **4**, PLUS LEFTOVERS
25 MINUTES TO MAKE
30 MINUTES TO COOK

CHICKEN HAINAN

200ML (7FL OZ) OLIVE OIL

2 LARGE ONIONS, FINELY SLICED

SEA SALT

8 CHICKEN THIGH FILLETS

500ML (18FL OZ) CHICKEN STOCK
(PAGE 101)

3CM (1¼IN) PIECE OF FRESH GINGER,
PEELED AND CUT INTO MATCHSTICKS

100G (3½OZ) BUNCH OF FRESH
CORIANDER

2 STAR ANISE

1 BUNCH OF SPRING ONIONS, SLICED
INTO 3CM (1¼IN) PIECES

1 TABLESPOON TOASTED SESAME OIL

250G (9OZ) SPRING GREENS, SAVOY
CABBAGE, CHARD, KALE OR
BROCCOLI, SHREDDED

300G (10½OZ) BASMATI RICE

4 TABLESPOONS DARK OR LIGHT SOY
SAUCE

4 TABLESPOONS RICE WINE OR MALT
VINEGAR

2 GREEN FINGER CHILLIES, SLICED

½ CUCUMBER, DESEEDED AND SLICED
INTO QUARTER MOONS

150G (5½OZ) CHERRY TOMATOES,
QUARTERED

1. Heat the oil in a frying pan and very gently fry the onions with a pinch of salt until they are golden brown and crisp. Remove with a slotted spoon and drain on kitchen paper.

2. Put the chicken in a pan and pour over the stock and 750ml (25fl oz) water, add the ginger, the stalks of the coriander, the star anise and half the spring onions. Bring to the boil and simmer for 15-20 minutes until the chicken is cooked. Scoop out the chicken and cut into small pieces. Put about half into a bowl for a leftover recipe such as Soul Soup (page 98) or Coconut + Chilli Chicken Pots (page 99), toss the remainder in the sesame oil and return to the pan with the greens, then simmer until just tender.

3. Meanwhile, cook the rice in boiling salted water for 10 minutes until tender. Drain and set aside.

4. Mix the soy with the vinegar and the chillies. Spoon the rice into 4 bowls. Use a slotted spoon to scoop the chicken and bits into the bowls and then pour over a ladleful of soup. Drizzle with the soy mixture and scatter with the cucumber, cherry tomatoes and crispy onions. Garnish with the remaining spring onions and coriander.

tip A great way to make this recipe if you have a bit more time is to simmer a whole chicken in the fragrant stock for an hour until it is cooked. This not only adds bags of extra flavour but gives you lots more leftover chook to make other recipes with.

ENOUGH LEFT OVER FOR:
SOUL SOUP (PAGE 98)
COCONUT + CHILLI CHICKEN POTS (PAGE 99) ≫——→

What is it about chicken soup that nourishes the soul? Whether it does have true medicinal properties or if it is just because it tastes so good, it is the perfect pick-me-up for when you are feeling run-down. The intense broth from the Hainan provides the perfect platform on which to build the ultimate leftovers soup.

SERVES **2**
5 MINUTES TO MAKE
10 MINUTES TO COOK

1 TABLESPOON OLIVE OIL

1 ONION, FINELY SLICED

2 CELERY STICKS, FINELY SLICED

500ML (18FL OZ) LEFTOVER CHICKEN
  HAINAN BROTH (PAGE 97)

100G (3½OZ) ANGEL HAIR PASTA,
  BROKEN INTO SMALL BITS

150G (5½OZ) SPRING GREENS, SAVOY OR
  POINTY CABBAGE, CHARD, KALE OR
  BROCCOLI, SHREDDED

A SMALL HANDFUL OF CHOPPED DILL

SOUL SOUP

1. Heat the oil in a saucepan and gently fry the onion and celery for 10 minutes until softened. Add the broth and 200ml (7fl oz) water and bring to the boil, then add the pasta and greens. Simmer until the pasta is tender (just a couple of minutes), then stir in the dill and serve. If you have any chicken left over from your Hainan, you can add that to the soup at the end too.

tip If you haven't cooked the Chicken Hainan (page 97), then use good-quality fresh chicken stock (page 101) and simmer with a 2cm (¾in) piece of chopped fresh ginger and a couple of star anise.

Pot pies are a great favourite of mine, as just about anything tastes good under a crust of golden crispy pastry. This one is packed full of spice and flavour with a rich hit of coconut. Shop-bought puff is a great standby to have in your freezer to transform your leftovers.

COCONUT + CHILLI CHICKEN POTS

SERVES **4**

15 MINUTES TO MAKE

30 MINUTES TO COOK

1 TABLESPOON OLIVE OIL

1 BUNCH OF SPRING ONIONS, FINELY CHOPPED

1 GARLIC CLOVE, FINELY SLICED

1 GREEN FINGER CHILLI, OR OTHER CHILLI, FINELY CHOPPED

250ML (9FL OZ) LEFTOVER CHICKEN HAINAN BROTH (PAGE 97)

1 TEASPOON CORNFLOUR

400ML (14FL OZ) CAN OF COCONUT MILK

250G (9OZ) SPRING GREENS, SAVOY OR POINTY CABBAGE, CHARD, KALE OR BROCCOLI, SHREDDED

4 LEFTOVER COOKED CHICKEN THIGHS (PAGE 97), CHOPPED

SEA SALT AND FRESHLY GROUND BLACK PEPPER

375G (13OZ) PACK READY-ROLLED ALL-BUTTER PUFF PASTRY

1 FREE-RANGE EGG, BEATEN

1. Heat the oil in a pan and gently fry the spring onions for a few minutes, then add the garlic and chilli and fry for a further minute. Mix a little broth with the cornflour until smooth, then add to the pan with the remaining broth. Add the coconut milk, greens and chicken and season. Remove from the heat and divide between 4 x 300ml (10fl oz) ovenproof pots.

2. Preheat the oven to 200°C/fan 180°C/400°F/gas 6. Unroll the pastry and cut out lids to fit your pots. Use the leftover pastry trimmings to fix the lids to the rims of your pots, then brush all over with beaten egg and bake for 20 minutes until puffed and golden.

tip If you haven't made the Chicken Hainan (page 97), then use 4 chopped chicken thigh fillets and simmer in 250ml (9fl oz) chicken stock with a star anise until cooked, then continue with the recipe as above.

A roast chicken is a universal joy. The transformation from humble bird to gloriously golden feast is wonderful to watch. Buy the best free-range chicken available as you can easily make three meals from the one purchase, so the cost is spread out and the flavour of the resulting roast is incomparable.

ROAST CHICKEN WITH LEMON + TARRAGON

SERVES **4**, PLUS LEFTOVERS
15 MINUTES TO MAKE
1 HOUR **25** MINUTES TO COOK

1 FREE-RANGE CHICKEN,
   WEIGHING ABOUT 2KG (4LB 8OZ)
2 TABLESPOONS UNSALTED BUTTER,
   SOFTENED
1 GARLIC CLOVE, CRUSHED
ZEST OF 2 LEMONS, PLUS JUICE OF 1
1 SMALL BUNCH OF TARRAGON
SEA SALT AND FRESHLY GROUND BLACK
   PEPPER
750G (1LB 10OZ) NUTTY NEW POTATOES
   (ANAYA OR PINK FIR APPLES ARE MY
   FAVOURITES)
150ML (5 FL OZ) DRY WHITE WINE
400ML (14 FL OZ) CHICKEN STOCK
   (SEE TIP)

tip To make chicken stock with the carcass, just break the bones into pieces and put in a deep pan with a chopped onion, carrot and celery stick (if you have them) and add any herbs, such as bay leaf, parsley stalks, sprigs of thyme or rosemary. Cover with water and simmer for 2 hours, skimming every so often. Strain and cool. Keep in the fridge for up to a week or freeze in small quantities.

1. Preheat the oven to 200°C/fan 180°C/400°F/gas 6. Take your chicken and use your fingers to separate the skin from the breast meat, working up under the skin from the neck end of the bird, being careful not to tear the skin.

2. Mix the butter with the garlic and lemon zest. Finely chop two-thirds of the tarragon and squidge that into the butter with plenty of sea salt and black pepper. Use your hands to push the butter up under the skin and smear it over the breast.

3. Put the chicken into a roasting tin, squeeze over the lemon juice and pop the lemon halves into the cavity. Scatter the potatoes around the outside and pour over the wine and 100ml (3½fl oz) of the stock.

4. Roast for at least 1 hour or until the chicken is golden and just cooked – when you pierce the thickest part of the bird (between the thigh and breast) with a knife, the juices should run clear. Place on a warmed platter and use a slotted spoon to put the potatoes around the outside. Leave to rest for at least 15 minutes, covered loosely in foil.

5. Put the tin with the cooking juices over a high heat, add the remaining stock and chopped tarragon and bubble for a few minutes, adding any juices from the resting chicken. Serve with the carved chicken.

6. When you have served the chicken, strip the carcass of all its remaining meat with your fingers and save any juices or gravy for leftover dishes.

ENOUGH LEFT OVER FOR:
ROAST CHICKEN + MUSHROOM RISOTTO (PAGE 102)
QUICK CHICKEN, PURPLE SPROUTING BROCCOLI +
   STICKY CHILLI STIR-FRY (PAGE 104) ⟶

If rice is my go-to staple ingredient, then risotto has to be my favourite rice dish. A good risotto should be creamy and soft, never sticky or heavy. This is the BEST mushroom risotto you will ever make, as testified by my photographer Laura and her husband Bob who, on eating it, instantly added it to his last meal list.

ROAST CHICKEN + MUSHROOM RISOTTO

SERVES **4**
30 MINUTES TO MAKE
30 MINUTES TO COOK

2 TABLESPOONS OLIVE OIL
1 SMALL ONION OR 2 BANANA
　SHALLOTS, FINELY SLICED
350G (12OZ) RISOTTO RICE
200ML (7FL OZ) WHITE WINE OR
　VERMOUTH OR VODKA
500-700ML (18FL OZ-1¼ PINTS) HOT
　CHICKEN STOCK (HOMEMADE STOCK
　– PAGE 101 – OR A PORCINI STOCK
　CUBE IS GREAT)
50G (1¾OZ) UNSALTED BUTTER
350G (12OZ) BUTTON, CHESTNUT OR
　FLAT MUSHROOMS, FINELY CHOPPED
150ML (5FL OZ) DOUBLE CREAM OR
　CRÈME FRAÎCHE
SEA SALT AND FRESHLY GROUND BLACK
　PEPPER
ABOUT 200-300G (7-10½OZ) LEFTOVER
　ROAST CHICKEN, SHREDDED, PLUS
　ANY LEFTOVER GRAVY (PAGE 101)
30G (1OZ) PARMESAN CHEESE, GRATED
A HANDFUL OF FINELY CHOPPED
　FLAT-LEAF PARSLEY

1. Heat the oil in a saucepan and gently fry the onion for 5-10 minutes until softened but not too coloured. Add the rice and toast in the oil and onion for 30 seconds until the grains become slightly translucent.

2. Splosh in the wine and stir vigorously until it is all absorbed. Then start adding your stock, a ladleful at a time, stirring and making sure each addition is absorbed before adding the next.

3. Meanwhile, melt the butter in a frying pan and fry the chopped mushrooms over a medium-high heat until golden brown. Add the cream or crème fraîche and season with sea salt and black pepper and bubble together, then whizz in a blender or mini processor until you have a paste.

4. Once the rice is almost cooked, add the mushroom paste and a little more seasoning to taste and stir in. Add a good ladleful of stock, the chicken and Parmesan and remove from the heat. Cover with a lid and leave it to stand for 5 minutes – this relaxes the rice and lets it become unctuous and silky. Add the parsley and serve.

tip If you haven't cooked the Roast Chicken with Lemon + Tarragon (page 101), you can roast 250g (9oz) chicken (breast, thigh or leg) in a hot oven (200°C/fan 180°C/400°F/gas 6) for 20 minutes while you cook the risotto, then use this for the finished dish.

Anything goes in this super speedy midweek supper – whatever vegetables and bits and pieces you have in your fridge and left over from your roast chicken will work brilliantly.

QUICK CHICKEN, PURPLE SPROUTING BROCCOLI + STICKY CHILLI STIR-FRY

SERVES **4**
10 MINUTES TO MAKE
10 MINUTES TO COOK

2 TABLESPOONS SUNFLOWER OR
   VEGETABLE OIL

2 GARLIC CLOVES, SLICED

2.5CM (1IN) PIECE OF FRESH GINGER,
   PEELED AND FINELY SLICED
   INTO MATCHSTICKS

1-2 RED CHILLIES, FINELY SLICED

STAR ANISE

300G (10½OZ) PURPLE SPROUTING
   BROCCOLI OR ANY OTHER GREENS,
   SUCH AS CABBAGE, PAK CHOI,
   CAVALO NERO OR CHINESE LEAF

ABOUT 200-300G (3½-7OZ) LEFTOVER
   ROAST CHICKEN (PAGE 101), CHOPPED

100-200G LEFTOVER ROAST POTATOES
   (PAGE 101), SLICED

1 TABLESPOON RICE WINE VINEGAR

2 TABLESPOONS CLEAR HONEY OR
   SWEET CHILLI DIPPING SAUCE

2 TABLESPOONS DARK OR LIGHT SOY
   SAUCE

A BIG HANDFUL OF CORIANDER,
   ROUGHLY CHOPPED

COOKED RICE AND LIME WEDGES,
   TO SERVE

1. Heat the oil in a wok or large frying pan over a high heat and very quickly speed-fry the garlic, ginger and chillies for 30 seconds. Add the star anise, broccoli and a splash of water (about 1–2 tablespoons) and cook in the steam, tossing gently for 2–3 minutes. Add the remaining ingredients except for the coriander.

2. Cook for a minute, tossing until coated in the sticky sauce, then add the coriander and serve with rice and lime wedges.

tip If you haven't cooked the Roast Chicken with Lemon + Tarragon (page 101), use 2 chicken breasts or 4 thigh fillets, meat sliced, and stir-fry quickly for 5–6 minutes at the start of the recipe.

Shoulder of lamb is one of the best slow-roasting joints as the fat and sinews melt into the meat until it is so soft you can shred it with a fork. The barbecue is a greatly underused bit of kit but, if you get the hang of using it for slow cooking, you will be out there in the depths of winter armed with your tongs and charcoal.

CHARGRILLED LAMB SHOULDER

SERVES 4-6, PLUS LEFTOVERS
15 MINUTES TO MAKE, PLUS
   MARINATING
2 HOURS 20 MINUTES TO COOK

1 LARGE SHOULDER OF LAMB,
   WEIGHING ABOUT 2-2.5KG
   (4LB 8OZ-5LB 8OZ)
500G (1LB 2OZ) GREEK YOGURT
4 GARLIC CLOVES, CRUSHED
4 SPRIGS OF ROSEMARY, LEAVES
   STRIPPED AND FINELY CHOPPED
3 CANNED/JARRED ANCHOVIES, FINELY
   CHOPPED
FINELY GRATED ZEST AND JUICE OF
   1 LEMON
1 TABLESPOON SOFT LIGHT BROWN
   SUGAR
SEA SALT AND FRESHLY GROUND BLACK
   PEPPER

1. Put the lamb shoulder in a dish and make incisions all over it with a sharp knife.

2. Mix the yogurt with the remaining ingredients and season well. Spread all over the lamb and leave to marinate for at least an hour or overnight if possible.

3. Light a kettle barbecue and get it nice and hot. Put the lamb on the barbecue and char the lamb on each side for 5-10 minutes. Transfer to a roasting tin lined with a large double layer of foil and pour in 200ml (7fl oz) water. Bring the foil around to enclose the lamb, then return to the barbecue and shut the lid. Cook for 2 hours, checking every so often and topping up with more water if it is drying out, until the meat is tender and falling from the bone.

tip This recipe is ideal to cook on a barbecue, but if you fancy doing it in the oven it is really simple. Just roast in a roasting tin lined with foil as above for 2½ hours at 160°C/fan 140°C/325°F/gas 3. Then uncover and increase the temperature to 220°C/fan 200°C/425°F/gas 7 and brown for 15 minutes.

ENOUGH LEFT OVER FOR:
FATTEH (PAGE 107)
LAMB KARAHI (PAGE 108) ⇢⟶

Meaning 'to crumble' in Arabic, fatteh is stale or toasted bread, crumbled and layered with other ingredients. A bit like the best Middle Eastern nacho dish you could imagine. Sweet tomatoes, richly spiced leftover lamb and lots of yogurt create a sumptuous leftovers dinner from almost entirely store cupboard ingredients.

SERVES **4**
25 MINUTES TO MAKE
45-50 MINUTES TO COOK

FATTEH

2 TABLESPOONS OLIVE OIL

1 LARGE ONION, FINELY SLICED

3 GARLIC CLOVES, CRUSHED

1 CINNAMON STICK

1 TEASPOON PAPRIKA

400G (14OZ) CAN OF CHOPPED
    TOMATOES

400G (14OZ) LEFTOVER CHARGRILLED
    LAMB SHOULDER (PAGE 105),
    SHREDDED

SEA SALT AND FRESHLY GROUND BLACK
    PEPPER

6 WHITE PITTA BREADS, OPENED OUT

25G (1OZ) UNSALTED BUTTER, MELTED

250ML (9FL OZ) GREEK YOGURT OR
    NATURAL YOGURT

50G (1¾OZ) TOASTED PINE NUTS

A HANDFUL OF CHOPPED CORIANDER,
    TO SCATTER

FOR THE RICE

GOOD KNOB OF UNSALTED BUTTER

1 ONION, FINELY CHOPPED

150G (5½OZ) BASMATI RICE

400G (14OZ) CAN OF CHICKPEAS,
    DRAINED AND RINSED

50G (1¾OZ) SULTANAS

1. Heat the oil in a saucepan and gently fry the onion for 10 minutes. Add the garlic, cinnamon stick and paprika and cook for a minute, then add the tomatoes and lamb. Season and bubble for 15 minutes until thickened.

2. Meanwhile, for the rice, melt the butter in a pan, add the onion and fry gently for 10 minutes until softened. Add the rice and stir to coat, then add the chickpeas and sultanas and 300ml (10fl oz) water. Season and cover, then simmer gently for 10–12 minutes until the rice is tender.

3. Brush the pitta breads with the melted butter and cut into triangles. Toast in a medium oven at 160°C/fan 140°C/325°F/gas 3 until golden and crisp.

4. Place the pitta breads on a platter and top with the rice, then spoon over the lamb mixture and finish with some dollops of yogurt, the toasted pine nuts and a scattering of coriander.

tip If you haven't made the Chargrilled Lamb Shoulder (page 105), then use 400g (14oz) minced lamb and cook it with the onion and spices at the start of the recipe until tender. It has a slightly different texture but is just as delicious.

A great simple curry to have at your fingertips, fast and no-nonsense, this always hits the spot. These flavours would be great with chicken or you could make this veggie by adding chickpeas instead of lamb.

SERVES **4**
10 MINUTES TO MAKE
35-45 MINUTES TO COOK

LAMB KARAHI

4 TABLESPOONS OLIVE OIL

2 AUBERGINES, CUT INTO CUBES

GOOD KNOB OF BUTTER

1 ONION, SLICED

2 GARLIC CLOVES, FINELY SLICED

2 TEASPOONS CUMIN SEEDS

2 TEASPOONS GROUND CORIANDER

1 TEASPOON GROUND TURMERIC

2 DRIED RED CHILLIES OR 1 TEASPOON
  DRIED CHILLI FLAKES

400G (14OZ) CAN OF CHOPPED
  TOMATOES

400G (14OZ) LEFTOVER CHARGRILLED
  LAMB SHOULDER (PAGE 105),
  SHREDDED

SEA SALT AND FRESHLY GROUND BLACK
  PEPPER

1 TEASPOON GARAM MASALA

1. Heat the oil in a saucepan and gently fry the aubergines for 10-15 minutes until really soft. Set aside. Add the butter to the pan and gently fry the onion for 10 minutes until softened. Add the garlic and spices and fry for a further minute.

2. Add the tomatoes, lamb and cooked aubergines with a good splash of water and plenty of seasoning and bubble for 15-20 minutes, then add the garam masala. Serve with rice.

tip If you haven't cooked the Chargrilled Lamb Shoulder (page 105), brown 400g (14oz) diced lamb leg steaks and use in step 2.

Rump cap, or *picanha* as it is known in Brazil, is still a little known cut over here. It is the cap of meat that normally sits on top of the whole rump – you get a little bit of it when you buy rump steak. Instead of slicing as part of the rump, it is removed and sold as a whole piece. It is like a steak roasting joint, meaning you get the best of both worlds.

SPICE-CRUSTED RUMP CAP WITH PUY LENTIL SALAD

SERVES **4**, PLUS LEFTOVERS
15 MINUTES TO MAKE
35 MINUTES TO COOK

2 TEASPOONS BLACK PEPPERCORNS

2 TEASPOONS SEA SALT

2 TEASPOONS CUMIN SEEDS

1 TEASPOON CORIANDER SEEDS

GOOD GRATING OF NUTMEG

PINCH OF DRIED CHILLI FLAKES

1.5KG (3LB 5OZ) WHOLE RUMP CAP

OLIVE OIL, TO DRIZZLE

FOR THE LENTILS

300G (10½OZ) PUY LENTILS

600ML (20FL OZ) CHICKEN STOCK
   (PAGE 101)

SEA SALT AND FRESHLY GROUND BLACK
   PEPPER

1 SWEET ONION, FINELY SLICED

1 TABLESPOON CIDER VINEGAR

3 TABLESPOONS EXTRA VIRGIN
   OLIVE OIL

A HANDFUL OF FLAT-LEAF PARSLEY,
   CHOPPED

1. Preheat the oven to 200°C/fan 180°C/400°F/gas 6. Mix the pepper, salt and spices together in a pestle and mortar and pound to a coarse mixture. Heat a heavy-based pan over a high heat, drizzle the beef with olive oil and sear briefly on all sides until golden. Press the spice crust all over the beef and put it in a roasting tin, then roast for 30–35 minutes until cooked but still pink inside – it should read 50–52°C (122–126°F) on a digital thermometer. Leave it to rest for at least 10 minutes before serving.

2. Meanwhile, put the lentils in a pan with the stock, season and bring to the boil. Simmer for 15–20 minutes until tender and the stock is absorbed. Drain any excess stock and tip the lentils into a bowl. Toss with the sweet onion. Mix the cider vinegar with plenty of sea salt and black pepper then whisk in the olive oil to make a glossy dressing. Pour over the lentils and toss together with the parsley. Serve with slices of rump cap.

tip If you can't get hold of a whole rump cap you can easily use a whole piece of sirloin steak instead, imagine 4–5 nice fat steaks together in a piece and you should have the right amount.

ENOUGH LEFT OVER FOR:
TAGLIATA (PAGE 112)
BEEF WITH BÉARNAISE SAUCE + CHIPS (PAGE 114) ⟫⟶

If I am honest I do love cold steak or roast beef on its own, with a smidge of mustard, but sometimes it's fun to mix things up and create something a bit more special. It doesn't take much to turn leftover steak into something fabulous like this tagliata.

SERVES **4**
5 MINUTES TO MAKE
2-3 MINUTES TO COOK

200G (7OZ) WILD ROCKET, WATERCRESS
   OR OTHER SPICY SALAD LEAVES
300G (10½OZ) LEFTOVER SPICE-
   CRUSTED RUMP CAP (PAGE 111),
   THINLY SLICED
120ML (4FL OZ) EXTRA VIRGIN OLIVE OIL
2 SPRIGS OF ROSEMARY
1 LARGE GARLIC CLOVE, BASHED
PARED ZEST OF ½ LEMON, PLUS JUICE
   OF 1 LEMON
PARMESAN SHAVINGS, TO SERVE

TAGLIATA

1. Put the rocket into a salad bowl and place the sliced beef on top.

2. Heat the oil in a pan over a very low heat and add the rosemary, garlic and lemon zest and leave to infuse for a couple of minutes. Remove from the heat and whisk in the lemon juice.

3. Spoon the dressing over the steak and leaves, scatter with Parmesan shavings and serve.

tip If you haven't cooked the Spice-crusted Rump Cap (page 111), then rub 2 x 150g (5½oz) rump or sirloin steaks with a little olive oil and sear for 1–2 minutes on each side until rare, then slice before you make the dressing.

Something as simple as a Béarnaise sauce and really good chips can transform leftover steak or roast beef into something sumptuous. Don't be afraid of Béarnaise sauce, this method is as easy as any I've ever tried.

· · · · · ········ · · · ···· · ········ · · ···· · · · · ··

SERVES **4**
30 MINUTES TO MAKE
50 MINUTES TO COOK

800G (1LB 12OZ) FLOURY POTATOES, SUCH AS KING EDWARD OR MARIS PIPER
40G (1½OZ) DRIPPING OR 3 TABLESPOONS OLIVE OIL
400G (14OZ) LEFTOVER SPICE-CRUSTED RUMP CAP (PAGE 111)

FOR THE BÉARNAISE
2 TABLESPOONS WHITE WINE VINEGAR
6 BLACK PEPPERCORNS
1 SHALLOT, FINELY CHOPPED
1 BUNCH OF TARRAGON, LEAVES STRIPPED AND CHOPPED, STALKS RESERVED
2 FREE-RANGE EGG YOLKS
SEA SALT AND FRESHLY GROUND BLACK PEPPER
220G (8OZ) COLD UNSALTED BUTTER, CUT INTO CUBES
LEMON JUICE, TO TASTE

BEEF WITH BÉARNAISE SAUCE + CHIPS

1. Preheat the oven to 200°C/fan 180°C/400°F/gas 6. Peel the potatoes and cut into whatever size and shape of chips you like – I love little cubes so you get extra golden crunchy bits. Drop into a pan of cold, salted water, bring to the boil and simmer for 3–5 minutes (depending on size) until parboiled. Drain and return to the pan over a low heat and toss gently to fluff up the edges.

2. Heat the dripping or oil in a roasting tin, then add the potatoes and toss to coat. Roast for 45–50 minutes, turning occasionally, until gorgeously golden and crisp.

3. Meanwhile, for the sauce, put the vinegar and 1 tablespoon of water into a small pan over a medium heat. Add the peppercorns, shallot and the tarragon stalks. Bubble until reduced to 2 teaspoons in volume. Sieve into a medium heatproof bowl.

4. Place the bowl over a pan of barely simmering water so the bottom doesn't touch the water. Add the egg yolks to the vinegar with some seasoning and whisk for 30 seconds. Gradually add the butter cubes, whisking all the time, allowing them to melt and become emulsified before adding the next couple. Keep going until you have used up all the butter and you have a glossy, thick sauce. Remove from the pan and keep whisking as you add the chopped tarragon and lemon juice to taste.

5. Remove the rump cap from the fridge 20 minutes before serving, slice and serve with the chips and Béarnaise sauce.

tip If you haven't cooked the Spice-crusted Rump Cap (page 111), sear 2 x 200g (7oz) sirloin or rump steaks in a drizzle of olive oil for 1–2 minutes on each side until rare, then slice.

On a cold day there is nothing as lovely as a big plateful of a rich meaty ragù. For me, beef shin has to be my favourite choice for a slow braise as its gelatinous nature adds a depth to the gravy that you just don't get with other cuts.

SLOW-COOKED BEEF RAGÙ

SERVES **4-6**, PLUS LEFTOVERS
30 MINUTES TO MAKE
3 HOURS TO COOK

OLIVE OIL, TO FRY

SEA SALT AND FRESHLY GROUND BLACK PEPPER

4 TABLESPOONS PLAIN FLOUR

1.5KG (3LB 5OZ) SHIN OF BEEF, CUT INTO LARGE 2-3CM (¾-1¼IN) CHUNKS

150G (5½OZ) COOKING CHORIZO, CUT INTO 1CM (½IN) PIECES

1 ONION, FINELY SLICED

1 CARROT, FINELY CHOPPED

2 CELERY STICKS, FINELY CHOPPED

2 BAY LEAVES

6 SPRIGS OF THYME

300ML (10FL OZ) WHITE WINE

400G (14OZ) CAN OF CHOPPED TOMATOES

2 TABLESPOONS TOMATO PURÉE, PLUS A SQUIDGE EXTRA

300ML (10FL OZ) BEEF OR CHICKEN STOCK (PAGE 101)

2 TEASPOONS SOFT LIGHT BROWN SUGAR

1. Take a large, flameproof casserole dish and heat the oil in the bottom. Season the flour, toss the chunks of beef in it and brown in batches in the hot oil, then remove with a slotted spoon. Once all the beef is browned, add the chorizo and brown all over.

2. Remove all but a couple of tablespoons of the oil from the casserole, then add the onion, carrot and celery and fry gently for 10 minutes. Return the meat to the pan and add the herbs and white wine. Bubble for a few minutes, then add the tomatoes, tomato purée, stock and sugar. Season and bring to the boil. Cover and reduce to a simmer and cook for 2–2½ hours until really tender and falling apart. Remove the lid for the last 45 minutes of cooking to reduce the sauce to a thick, glossy gravy.

ENOUGH LEFT OVER FOR:
BEEF + BARLEY SOUP (PAGE 118)
SMOKY BEEF EMPANADAS (PAGE 119) »⟶

A great way of using up leftover braises, stews and ragùs is to turn them into soup. The beauty is they are halfway there already. A little more stock and a few extra ingredients can transform last night's supper into a wonderful winter lunch.

SERVES **4**
10 MINUTES TO MAKE
40-50 MINUTES TO COOK

1 TABLESPOON OLIVE OIL

1 LARGE ONION, FINELY CHOPPED

1 SPRIG OF ROSEMARY

ABOUT 400G (14OZ) LEFTOVER SLOW-
    COOKED BEEF RAGÙ (PAGE 115)

1 LITRE (1¾ PINTS) BEEF STOCK (FRESH
    IS BEST OR FROM A CUBE)

150G (5½OZ) PEARL BARLEY

CRUSTY BREAD, TO SERVE

BEEF + BARLEY SOUP

1. Heat the oil in a deep pan and gently fry the onion and rosemary for 10 minutes until lovely and soft. Add your leftover beef ragù, the stock and pearl barley and cook gently for 30–40 minutes until the pearl barley is cooked and tender. Serve with hunks of crusty bread.

tip If you haven't made the Slow-cooked Beef Ragù (page 115), don't worry, you can still make this wonderful soup. Brown off 300g (10½oz) diced braising steak. Add ½ teaspoon each of smoked hot and sweet paprika to the frying onions, then add the steak and stock with a squidge of tomato purée and a 250g (9oz) can of chopped tomatoes and simmer gently for 30 minutes before adding the pearl barley and another slosh of beef stock. Simmer for a further 30–40 minutes until the pearl barley is tender.

The pasty of the Spanish-speaking world, empanadas are great as a portable lunch or as a tasty leftovers supper with a big green salad.

MAKES **6**
40 MINUTES TO MAKE, PLUS CHILLING
25-30 MINUTES TO COOK

SMOKY BEEF EMPANADAS

FOR THE FILLING

1 TABLESPOON OLIVE OIL

1 LARGE ONION, FINELY SLICED

2 TEASPOONS SMOKED PAPRIKA

ABOUT 300G (10½OZ) LEFTOVER SLOW-
    COOKED BEEF RAGÙ (PAGE 115)

200G (7OZ) FROZEN PEAS, DEFROSTED

2-3 TABLESPOONS SOURED CREAM,
    GREEK YOGURT OR CRÈME FRAÎCHE

FOR THE PASTRY

250G (9OZ) PLAIN FLOUR

½ TEASPOON FINE SEA SALT

100G (3½OZ) COLD UNSALTED BUTTER,
    CUBED

1 FREE-RANGE EGG, BEATEN

1 TEASPOON WHITE WINE VINEGAR

tip If you haven't made the Slow-cooked Beef Ragù (page 115), add 300g (10½oz) minced beef to the frying onion and brown. Add 1 teaspoon of paprika, a 250g (9oz) can of chopped tomatoes and a splash of beef stock. Simmer for 30 minutes until thickened, then add the peas and soured cream and leave to cool.

1. To make the pastry, tip the flour and salt into a bowl and rub the cold butter into it with your fingers until it resembles breadcrumbs. Mix half the beaten egg with 2 tablespoons of cold water and the vinegar, add to the bowl and mix in quickly. Bring together with your hands and knead very briefly to make a smooth dough. Shape into a disc, wrap in clingfilm and chill for at least 30 minutes.

2. For the filling, heat the oil in a pan and gently fry the onion for 10 minutes. Add the paprika and cook for 30 seconds, then add the leftover ragù and peas and cook for 10 minutes, breaking the pieces of beef up with a wooden spoon. Spread on to a tray to cool. Mix in the soured cream, yogurt or crème fraîche.

3. Divide the pastry into 6 even-sized pieces and roll into balls. Roll each ball out into a disc and use a cutter or small plate to cut them into circles 16cm (6¼in) in diameter. Discard any trimmings.

4. Preheat the oven to 200°C/fan 180°C/400°F/gas 6. Cover all but one of the discs with a slightly damp tea towel to stop them drying out. Spoon a dollop of the filling mixture into the centre of the uncovered pastry circle, then brush the edges with a little water and fold them in half to enclose the filling in a semicircle. Press the edges to seal and crimp with your fingers or a fork.

5. Place on a baking sheet lined with nonstick baking paper and repeat with the remaining pastry and filling. Then brush with the remaining beaten egg and bake for 25-30 minutes until golden brown. Serve warm or at room temperature.

Boy, oh boy are these ribs the dawg's proverbials! With so little effort required on your part to make these amazing beauties, it's almost embarrassing! I'd go so far as to say this might be the best rib recipe I have ever written.

STICKY BRAISED SHORT RIBS

SERVES 4, PLUS LEFTOVERS

20 MINUTES TO MAKE, PLUS MARINATING

4 HOURS TO COOK

2KG (4LB 8OZ) BEEF SHORT RIBS

200ML (7FL OZ) LIGHT SOY SAUCE

200ML (7FL OZ) DARK SOY SAUCE

300G (10½OZ) SOFT LIGHT BROWN SUGAR

A GOOD SQUIDGE OF CLEAR HONEY

6 GARLIC CLOVES, BASHED

5CM (2IN) PIECE OF FRESH GINGER, PEELED AND SLICED

2 STAR ANISE

2 RED CHILLIES, FINELY SLICED

4 TABLESPOONS RICE WINE VINEGAR

1. Put the ribs into a shallow, non-metallic dish. Mix the soy sauces with 250g (9oz) of the sugar, the honey, garlic, ginger, star anise and chillies and pour over the ribs. Cover and marinate in the fridge for at least 3 hours or overnight if possible.

2. Preheat the oven to 160°C/fan 140°C/325°F/gas 3. Transfer the ribs and their marinade to a roasting tin, cover with foil and roast for 3–4 hours until the meat is very tender and falling off the bone. Check on them every so often and add a splash of water if they are getting dry. At this point you can leave the ribs to cool in the marinade and finish the next day.

3. When ready to finish, preheat the oven to 200°C/fan 180°C/400°F/gas 6. Pour off the marinade into a pan, add the rice wine vinegar and the remaining sugar and bubble to thicken to a glossy glaze. Put the ribs into the oven with a good drizzle of the glaze and roast, glazing and turning every 10 minutes, for 30 minutes or so until you have sticky, rich and sexy ribs. Serve with any leftover glaze.

ENOUGH LEFT OVER FOR:
THAI BEEF SALAD (PAGE 122)
BEEF SUMMER ROLLS (PAGE 124) »——→

Big, bold and beautiful, this is a salad to remember. Rather than the usual rare steak, I thought that using leftover sticky sweet rib meat would be perfect in such a zing-filled salad, and I was right!

SERVES **4**
15 MINUTES TO MAKE

THAI BEEF SALAD

1 CUCUMBER

2 CARROTS

100G (3½OZ) RADISHES

150G (5½OZ) MANGE TOUT, SUGAR
   SNAPS OR PEAS

100G (3½OZ) CHERRY TOMATOES,
   QUARTERED

½ BUNCH OF SPRING ONIONS, FINELY
   SLICED

2 BABY GEM OR OTHER CRUNCHY
   LETTUCES

1 SMALL BUNCH OF CORIANDER,
   ROUGHLY CHOPPED

250–300G (9–10½OZ) LEFTOVER STICKY
   BRAISED SHORT RIBS (PAGE 121),
   MEAT SHREDDED

2 TABLESPOONS SALTED PEANUTS,
   CHOPPED

FOR THE DRESSING

JUICE OF 2 LIMES

1 TABLESPOON FISH SAUCE

1 TABLESPOON DARK OR LIGHT SOY
   SAUCE

2 TEASPOONS SOFT LIGHT BROWN
   SUGAR OR PALM SUGAR

1 RED CHILLI, FINELY SLICED

2 TABLESPOONS SESAME OIL

1. Use a potato peeler to slice the cucumber and carrots into ribbons (or you can julienne the carrots if you prefer). Finely slice the radishes and mangetout or sugar snaps and toss together in a big bowl with the cherry tomatoes and spring onions.

2. Cut the baby gem into wedges and toss with the salad. Scatter over the coriander and shredded beef.

3. Mix all the ingredients for the dressing together in a small bowl and pour over the top of the salad, scatter with the peanuts and serve immediately.

tip If you haven't cooked the Sticky Braised Short Ribs (page 121), you can sear a 200–250g (7–9oz) sirloin steak over a high heat for 1–2 minutes on each side. Mix 3 tablespoons of dark or light soy sauce with 1 tablespoon of soft light brown sugar, 1 tablespoon of rice wine vinegar and 1 chopped red chilli together in a saucepan over a medium heat and bubble until slightly thickened. Slice the beef and pour over the sauce, then leave to stand while you make the salad.

These fresh and vibrant summer rolls are a great dish to make for friends, they look really impressive, but actually are so simple and you can prepare them in advance and keep chilled. Every bite is a wonderful burst of flavour.

BEEF SUMMER ROLLS

100G (3½OZ/1 SLAB) RICE VERMICELLI
   NOODLES OR OTHER RICE NOODLES
A HANDFUL OF CORIANDER, LEAVES
   PICKED
A FEW SPRIGS OF MINT, LEAVES
   PICKED
A HANDFUL OF THAI OR PERILLA BASIL,
   LEAVES PICKED
1 CARROT, CUT INTO MATCHSTICKS
½ CUCUMBER, CUT INTO MATCHSTICKS
½ BUTTERHEAD LETTUCE, BABY GEM OR
   OTHER LETTUCE, SHREDDED
300G (10½OZ) LEFTOVER STICKY
   BRAISED SHORT RIBS (PAGE 121),
   MEAT SHREDDED
16 RICE PAPER WRAPPERS OR
   LETTUCE LEAVES

FOR THE DIPPING SAUCE
1 TABLESPOON SOFT LIGHT BROWN
   SUGAR
JUICE OF 1 LIME
1 TABLESPOON FISH SAUCE
1 GREEN FINGER CHILLI, FINELY SLICED

1. To cook the noodles, put them in a heatproof bowl and pour over a kettleful of boiling water and leave for 3–4 minutes until al dente. Drain and run under cold water to stop them cooking, then drain well. Set aside.

2. Put the herbs, vegetables and meat into small bowls. Have a shallow dish of warm water to soften the rice wrappers and a clean tea towel in front of you on a chopping board.

3. Dip a wrapper in water and when it starts to feel silky and soft, remove it and place on the tea towel. Start by placing a few herbs in a line in the middle of your wrapper (or lettuce leaf), about halfway down. Top this line of herbs with some of each of the remaining ingredients (including the noodles), being careful not to overfill.

4. Fold the sides in, then fold the top down to cover the filling and roll up. You should end up with a layer of herbs along the top of your roll.

5. Repeat until you have used up all the ingredients. Mix the dipping sauce ingredients together in a small bowl and serve straight away.

tip If you haven't cooked the Sticky Braised Short Ribs (page 121), sear a 250g (9oz) sirloin steak for 1-2 minutes on each side until medium-rare. Rest for 5 minutes, then thinly slice and use as above.

An almost magical transformation occurs when you slow cook pork until the tender shreds of meat fall apart, full of flavour and silky smooth to eat, hardly a tooth is required except for the crackling. But it's the crackling that seals the deal, making this a truly great roast.

SERVES **4–6**, PLUS LEFTOVERS
15 MINUTES TO MAKE
4–5 HOURS TO COOK

SLOW-ROAST JUNIPER + FENNEL SEED PORK BELLY

3–4KG (6LB 8OZ–8LB 13OZ) PIECE OF OUTDOOR-REARED PORK BELLY, RIBS REMOVED BUT RETAINED AND SKIN SCORED
3 RED ONIONS, CUT INTO THIN WEDGES
2 TEASPOONS JUNIPER BERRIES, ROUGHLY CRUSHED
DRIZZLE OF OLIVE OIL
1 TABLESPOON SEA SALT FLAKES
1 TABLESPOON GREEN FENNEL SEEDS
300ML (10FL OZ) DRY CIDER

1. Preheat the oven to 220°C/fan 200°C/425°F/gas 7. Put the ribs of the pork belly into a roasting tin, scatter with the onions and juniper berries and drizzle with a little oil. Use the bones as a trivet for the belly to sit on. Mix the salt with the fennel seeds and press all over the skin.

2. Roast for 30 minutes, then reduce the temperature to 150°C/fan 130°C/300°F/gas 2 and cook for 4–5 hours until really tender. Increase the temperature to 220°C/fan 200°C/425°F/gas 7 for 5–10 minutes to crackle the skin at the end if you need to.

3. Remove from the oven and transfer to a warmed serving plate. Put the roasting tin with the ribs over a low heat and add the cider. Bubble and scrape all the yummy bits from the ribs into the gravy. Serve with the pork belly.

tip Using the ribs as a trivet is a great way to add extra flavour to your gravy, but you also get perfectly slow-cooked ribs as an extra leftover if you don't add them to your gravy. Either eat them cold with a slaw and baked potatoes or you could trim the meat off them to use in other recipes.

ENOUGH LEFT OVER FOR:
GOULASH (PAGE 128)
SHREDDED PORK + APPLE BUNS (PAGE 130) ⟫⟶

The beauty of this dish is that all the slow cooking has already been done for you. I've added beetroot to my goulash which isn't traditional, but I love its earthy sweet flavour against the warmth of the spices.

2 TABLESPOONS OLIVE OIL

2 ONIONS, FINELY SLICED

2 RED PEPPERS, DESEEDED AND SLICED

1 TABLESPOON SWEET PAPRIKA

2 TEASPOONS HOT PAPRIKA

2 TEASPOONS CARAWAY SEEDS

GOOD SQUIDGE OF TOMATO PURÉE

500G (1LB 2OZ) LEFTOVER SLOW-ROAST
    JUNIPER + FENNEL SEED PORK BELLY
    (PAGE 127), SHREDDED

500ML (18FL OZ) BEEF STOCK (FRESH IS
    BEST OR FROM A CUBE)

300G (10½OZ) NEW POTATOES, SWEET
    POTATOES OR BUTTERNUT SQUASH
    FLESH, CHOPPED

3 BEETROOTS, PEELED AND CHOPPED
    INTO SMALL PIECES

SOURED CREAM AND CHOPPED
    PARSLEY, TO SERVE

GOULASH

1. Heat the oil in a pan and gently fry the onions and red peppers for 10 minutes until softened.

2. Add the spices and tomato purée and fry for a further few minutes before adding the pork, stock, potatoes and beetroot. Bring to a simmer and cook for 15–20 minutes until the potatoes and beetroot are tender. Serve with dollops of soured cream and plenty of chopped parsley.

tip Instead of leftover pork belly (page 127), you can use 400g (14oz) sliced pork tenderloin quick-fried in a little olive oil at the start of the recipe.

Who says that a burger has to be made of mince? The tangy apples are the perfect foil for the leftover roast pork. Add a lick of yogurt or soured cream for an extra something.

SERVES **4**

5 MINUTES TO MAKE

25 MINUTES TO COOK

1 TABLESPOON OLIVE OIL

1 RED ONION, FINELY SLICED

2 APPLES, SUCH AS COX, PEELED, CORED AND CUT INTO WEDGES

1 TEASPOON SMOKED SWEET PAPRIKA

2 TEASPOONS SOFT LIGHT BROWN SUGAR

2 TABLESPOONS TOMATO KETCHUP

1 TABLESPOON WORCESTERSHIRE SAUCE

400G (14OZ) LEFTOVER SLOW-ROAST JUNIPER + FENNEL SEED PORK BELLY (PAGE 127), SHREDDED

BUNS OR BREAD, TO SERVE

SHREDDED PORK + APPLE BUNS

1. Heat the oil in a pan over a medium heat and fry the onion for 10 minutes until soft.

2. Add the apples and fry for 5 minutes before adding the remaining ingredients and a splash of water. Cook for 10 minutes until the pork is heated through and sticky, then spoon into buns and serve.

tip If you haven't cooked the Slow-roast Juniper + Fennel Seed Pork Belly (page 127), you can make these into pork sloppy joes instead. Add 300g (10½oz) minced pork to the pan with the onion and fry until brown before adding the remaining ingredients. Spoon the minced pork mixture into soft buns and serve with salad.

A pan full of golden, sizzling pork chops is a wonderful sight. The key to a fabulous chop is to not overcook it – it should be juicy and tender and almost a little pink in the middle before you eat it.

PAN-ROASTED PORK CHOPS WITH APPLES + ONIONS

SERVES **4**, PLUS LEFTOVERS
10 MINUTES TO MAKE
30 MINUTES TO COOK

4 LARGE OUTDOOR-REARED PORK
   CHOPS
1 TABLESPOON OLIVE OIL, PLUS EXTRA
   FOR BRUSHING
SEA SALT AND FRESHLY GROUND BLACK
   PEPPER
A HANDFUL OF SAGE LEAVES
2 ONIONS, FINELY SLICED
2-3 APPLES, PEELED, CORED AND CUT
   INTO WEDGES
100ML (3½FL OZ) CHICKEN STOCK
   (PAGE 101)

1. Preheat the oven to 200°C/fan 180°C/400°F/gas 6. Brush the pork chops with some oil and season well. Heat an ovenproof frying or sauté pan over a high heat and seal the pork chops on both sides until browned. Set aside.

2. Heat the oil in the pan and add the sage, onions and apples and fry for 5 minutes until they start to colour. Put the pork chops on top, splash in the stock, then transfer to the oven and cook for 15–20 minutes until the pork is cooked and the onions and apples are sticky and tender.

3. Leave the pork to rest for 10 minutes, then slice the meat from the bones, keeping the bones, and serve with the roasted onions and apples.

tip Although this recipe is for 4 pork chops, you will find that by slicing the meat from the bones, you will have more than enough for the main recipe and for leftovers (see pages 134 and 135).

ENOUGH LEFT OVER FOR:
SPICED PORK WITH HARISSA CHICKPEAS (PAGE 134)
RAINBOW SALAD (PAGE 135) ➤━━➤

There are a lot of fantastic chilli pastes and sauces from around the world, from the trendy and exciting sriracha and gochujang to the good old favourite Tabasco, but harissa is one of the best. It is so handy to have a jar in the fridge to pep up leftovers. I prefer rose harissa as it has a slightly more delicate flavour.

1 TABLESPOON OLIVE OIL

1 ONION, FINELY SLICED

2 GARLIC CLOVES, CRUSHED

JUICE OF 1 LEMON

1 RED ONION, FINELY SLICED

SEA SALT AND FRESHLY GROUND BLACK
    PEPPER

300G (10½OZ) LEFTOVER PAN-ROASTED
    PORK CHOPS (PAGE 131)

1 TABLESPOON ROSE HARISSA

2 X 400G (14OZ) CANS OF CHICKPEAS,
    DRAINED AND RINSED

SPLASH OF CHICKEN STOCK (PAGE 101)
    OR WATER

A HANDFUL OF CHOPPED FLAT-LEAF
    PARSLEY OR CORIANDER, TO FINISH

NATURAL YOGURT, TO DOLLOP

SPICED PORK WITH HARISSA CHICKPEAS

1. Heat the oil in a pan and gently fry the onion for 10 minutes. Add the garlic and fry for 30 seconds. Squeeze half the lemon juice over the red onion with some seasoning in a bowl and set aside to soften.

2. Meanwhile, remove any meat from the bones of the pork chops. Add this and the other sliced pork to the pan with the harissa and toss to coat. Add the chickpeas and stock or water, season and simmer for 5–10 minutes.

3. Add the remaining lemon juice to the chickpea mixture. Serve the chickpea mixture with the red onion, scattered with herbs and splodged with yogurt.

tip If you haven't cooked the Pan-roasted Pork Chops (page 131), slice 300g (10½oz) pork steaks or tenderloin and fry in a little olive oil until just cooked. Add a splash of cider or stock and a few sage leaves and simmer for a couple of minutes, then continue as above.

The idea behind a rainbow salad is that anything goes, pack in as many different coloured vegetables as you can. This can be a winter or a summer salad, and is just as delicious with kale and beetroot as it is with sliced asparagus, peas and beans.

2 BEETROOTS, PEELED

2 CARROTS, PEELED

1 CUCUMBER

½ RED OR WHITE CABBAGE

A FEW SPRING ONIONS

300G (10½OZ) LEFTOVER PAN-ROASTED PORK CHOPS (PAGE 131)

1 TEASPOON OLIVE OIL

DRIZZLE OF CLEAR HONEY

A HANDFUL OF MIXED NUTS AND SEEDS, SUCH AS SUNFLOWER SEEDS, HAZELNUTS AND ALMONDS

FOR THE DRESSING

JUICE OF ½ LEMON

SEA SALT AND FRESHLY GROUND BLACK PEPPER

PINCH OF CASTER SUGAR

2 TEASPOONS DIJON MUSTARD

3 TABLESPOONS EXTRA VIRGIN OLIVE OIL

1 TABLESPOON WALNUT OIL

RAINBOW SALAD

1. Finely slice your veggies however you like, use a potato peeler to make ribbons, slice into batons, grate, or finely slice, whatever takes your fancy. Toss them all together in a bowl.

2. Remove any meat from the pork chop bones and add to any leftover slices of pork. Heat the oil in a pan over a medium heat and add the pork and honey and toss together until warm, then add to the salad bowl with the mixed nuts and seeds.

3. To make the dressing, whisk the lemon juice with some sea salt, black pepper and the sugar, then gradually whisk in the mustard, then the oils. Pour over the salad and toss together, then serve.

tip This really is an utterly versatile salad so if you don't have leftover pork chops (page 131), you could slice and fry pork tenderloin, pork escalope or even minced pork to make this recipe.

VANILLA CRÈME ANGLAISE
MOUSSELINE ICING
PORTUGUESE CUSTARD TARTS

BERRY COMPOTE
BERRY + LIME POTS
BERRY RIPPLE ICE CREAM

APPLE + PECAN CRUMBLE
CRUMBLE CUPCAKES
APPLE + PECAN CRUMBLE TART

STAR ANISE + HONEY POACHED PEARS
PEAR TARTE FINE
UPSIDE DOWN PEAR + ALMOND CAKES

STICKY ALMOND + HONEY TART
SEMIFREDDO SLICE
STUFFED BAKED APPLES

CARDAMOM + CINNAMON BUNS
CARDAMOM BUN + CREAM PUDDING
PAIN PERDU

RICH CHOCOLATE MOUSSE
MINI CHOC 'N' NUT ICE CREAMS
CHOCOLATE FRIDGE CAKE

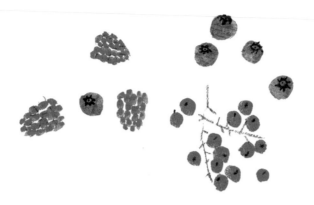

SWEET

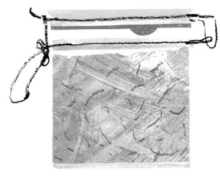

My favourite pudding when I was younger was cold banana custard – and my love of custard has never dimmed. If I am honest I like my custard on its own with a spoon, but I realize most other people prefer it with pudding!

SERVES **4**, PLUS LEFTOVERS
5 MINUTES TO MAKE
20 MINUTES TO COOK

VANILLA CRÈME ANGLAISE

300ML (10FL OZ) WHOLE MILK

300ML (10FL OZ) DOUBLE CREAM

1 VANILLA POD, SPLIT IN HALF
   LENGTHWAYS

4 FREE-RANGE EGG YOLKS

50G (1¾OZ) CASTER SUGAR

1 TEASPOON CORNFLOUR

1. Pour the milk and cream into a saucepan, scrape the seeds from the vanilla pod and add to the pan with the pod itself. Heat until almost boiling.

2. Meanwhile, beat the egg yolks, sugar and cornflour together in a heatproof bowl until smooth, pour the hot milk mixture over and stir well. Clean the pan and return the mixture to it.

3. Cook over a low heat, stirring constantly with a wooden spoon, until the mixture thickens and coats the back of the spoon.

tip Serve with tarts, such as the Sticky Almond + Honey Tart (page 159), pies, crumbles and steamed puddings.

ENOUGH LEFT OVER FOR:
MOUSSELINE ICING (PAGE 140)
PORTUGUESE CUSTARD TARTS (PAGE 142) ⇢⟶

Having made many wedding cakes in my time I am always searching for the ultimate icing – rich and sweet but stable and not cloying. I think this is it.

2 EGG WHITES
100G (3½OZ) ICING SUGAR
125G (4½OZ) UNSALTED BUTTER,
  SOFTENED
100ML (3½FL OZ) LEFTOVER VANILLA
  CRÈME ANGLAISE (PAGE 139)

MOUSSELINE ICING

1. Put the egg whites and icing sugar in a heatproof bowl and place over a pan of simmering water. Whisk with a hand-held electric whisk until you have a thick meringue mixture that holds its shape. Remove from the heat and whisk off the heat until cool.

2. In a separate bowl, beat the butter and crème anglaise together until really light and fluffy. Gradually add the meringue, a little at a time, beating in until you have a thick, smooth icing. Use to decorate one 20cm (8in) cake or a batch of cupcakes.

tip If you didn't make the Vanilla Crème Anglaise (page 139), you can instead make a classic mousseline icing using 175g (6oz) unsalted butter and a little vanilla extract.

Pastéis de nata are heavenly mouthfuls of light, flaky pastry with rich, caramelized custard. This is a cheat's version but is just as delicious as the real deal.

MAKES **12**
20 MINUTES TO MAKE
20 MINUTES TO COOK

250ML (9FL OZ) LEFTOVER VANILLA
    CRÈME ANGLAISE (PAGE 139)
50ML (2FL OZ) DOUBLE CREAM
1 TEASPOON CORNFLOUR, PLUS
    EXTRA TO DUST
25G (1OZ) CASTER SUGAR
1 FREE-RANGE EGG
GOOD GRATING OF NUTMEG
320G (11¼OZ) PACK READY-ROLLED
    ALL-BUTTER PUFF PASTRY

PORTUGUESE CUSTARD TARTS

1. Put the crème anglaise in a bowl and whisk the cream and cornflour together, then add to the bowl with the caster sugar, egg and nutmeg and whisk. Set aside.

2. Unroll the puff pastry on to a lightly cornfloured surface and roll out until 2mm (⅛in) thick. Roll the pastry up like a Swiss roll and slice into 12 even pieces.

3. Place each piece on its end (so you can see the rolls) and squash flat. Then put each piece into the hole of a 12-hole muffin tin and push up the sides with your fingers.

4. Preheat the oven to 240°C/fan 220°C/475°F/gas 9 or as hot as your oven will go. Pour the custard into the pastry cases, then bake for 15–20 minutes until the pastry is cooked and the tops are starting to scorch. Leave to cool in the tin for a few minutes before removing.

tip If you don't have any leftover Vanilla Crème Anglaise (page 139), you can mix 3 free-range egg yolks with 250g (9oz) crème fraîche and a little vanilla extract and grated nutmeg to taste.

Midsummer brings with it a plethora of wonderful berries, both familiar and unfamiliar. I would say use any berries in this glorious compote, except strawberries – cooked strawberries tend to be mushy and are much better savoured straight from the punnet with cream.

SERVES **4**, PLUS LEFTOVERS
5 MINUTES TO MAKE
10-20 MINUTES TO COOK

BERRY COMPOTE

600G (1LB 5OZ) MIXED BLACKBERRIES
 AND RASPBERRIES
250G (9OZ) MIXED BLACK, WHITE AND
 REDCURRANTS
60G (2¼OZ) CASTER SUGAR
1 VANILLA POD, SPLIT IN HALF
 LENGTHWAYS
50ML (2FL OZ) CRÈME DE CASSIS
 (OPTIONAL)

1. Put all the ingredients into a saucepan and heat gently until the sugar has dissolved, then bubble for 10–20 minutes until the fruit has started to break down and release all its juices. Remove from the heat and cool.

2. Serve with natural yogurt and granola or on top of creamy porridge.

ENOUGH LEFT OVER FOR:
BERRY + LIME POTS (PAGE 146)
BERRY RIPPLE ICE CREAM (PAGE 147) ⟫⟶

I love the texture of these little set creams, or possets.
Such a simple dessert but very elegant.

SERVES **4**

5 MINUTES TO MAKE, PLUS
    CHILLING

5 MINUTES TO COOK

BERRY + LIME POTS

400ML (14FL OZ) DOUBLE CREAM

120G (4¼OZ) CASTER SUGAR

JUICE OF 6 LIMES, PLUS THE ZEST OF 2

150G (5½OZ) LEFTOVER BERRY COMPOTE
    (PAGE 145)

1. Put the cream and sugar in a saucepan over a low heat and cook until the sugar has dissolved. Increase the heat and boil for 2–3 minutes, then remove from the heat and add the lime juice and zest.

2. Spoon half the mixture into four glasses, top each with a spoonful of the compote, then top with the remaining lime cream and chill for an hour before serving.

tip Without any leftover Berry Compote (page 145), you can simmer 150g (5½oz) mixed berries with 2 tablespoons of caster sugar (or to taste) until softened, then cool completely and use as above.

On a hot day nothing is nicer than a wafer cone piled high with ice cream. Berry ripple is a particular favourite of mine, although I don't think anything can quite pip mint choc chip to the top spot!

SERVES 4
30 MINUTES TO MAKE, PLUS CHILLING AND FREEZING
20 MINUTES TO COOK

400ML (14FL OZ) WHOLE MILK
6 FREE-RANGE EGG YOLKS
350G (12OZ) CASTER SUGAR
400G (14OZ) LEFTOVER BERRY COMPOTE (PAGE 145)
600ML (20FL OZ) DOUBLE CREAM

BERRY RIPPLE ICE CREAM

1. Bring the milk to the boil in a saucepan. In a heatproof bowl, whisk the egg yolks and sugar together until really pale, fluffy and thick and holding a ribbon when you lift the beaters out.

2. Pour the hot milk over the egg mixture and stir well. Clean the pan and pour the custard mixture back into it. Put over a medium-low heat and cook, stirring, until you have a thick custard that coats the back of a spoon. Leave to cool, cover with clingfilm, then chill overnight.

3. Put the leftover compote into a pan and bubble to reduce to a thick, jammy consistency. Set aside to cool.

4. Stir the cream into the custard and pour into an ice-cream maker. Churn until frozen. If you don't have an ice-cream maker, pour the mixture into a shallow, freezerproof, lidded container and freeze for 1–2 hours until almost solid, then scrape into a food processor and blend briefly until smooth. Return to the container and freeze once more. Repeat this procedure once or twice until the mixture is very smooth.

5. Scoop the frozen ice cream into a shallow, freezerproof, lidded container, drizzle the compote all over and ripple with a fork. Freeze for at least 6 hours or overnight if possible.

tip Without any leftover Berry Compote (page 145), you can simmer 400g (14oz) mixed berries with 4 tablespoons of caster sugar (or to taste) until softened, then increase the heat and bubble until thickened and jammy. Cool completely, then continue as above.

Crumbles are the king of winter comfort puddings and for good reason. Nestled underneath a golden, nutty crumb is soft and sharp apple, steaming and begging to be smothered with sweet custard.

SERVES **4**, PLUS LEFTOVERS
20 MINUTES TO MAKE
40-50 MINUTES TO COOK

APPLE + PECAN CRUMBLE

2 BRAMLEY APPLES

5-6 COX APPLES

JUICE OF 1 LEMON

100G (3½OZ) CASTER SUGAR

GOOD PINCH OF GROUND CINNAMON

GRATING OF NUTMEG

200G (7OZ) UNSALTED BUTTER, CUBED

175G (6OZ) PLAIN FLOUR

150G (5½OZ) PECANS, FINELY CHOPPED

75G (2¾OZ) DEMERARA SUGAR

40G (1½OZ) SOFT BROWN SUGAR
  (LIGHT OR DARK)

1 TEASPOON FLAKY SEA SALT

CREAM, CUSTARD OR VANILLA ICE
  CREAM, TO SERVE

1. Peel and core the apples, cut into small chunks and put in a pie or ovenproof dish. Add the lemon juice, caster sugar, spices and 50g (1¾oz) of the butter and mix together.

2. Preheat the oven to 160°C/fan 140°C/325°F/gas 3. Toss the remaining butter with the flour in a bowl and rub together with your fingertips until the mixture resembles breadcrumbs. Add the pecans, demerara and soft brown sugar and salt and mix well, then scatter over the top of the apples. Bake for 40-50 minutes until golden and bubbling. Serve with cream or vanilla ice cream.

ENOUGH LEFT OVER FOR:
CRUMBLE CUPCAKES (PAGE 150)
APPLE + PECAN CRUMBLE TART (PAGE 152) »——→

With just a big spoonful of leftover crumble you can make these wonderful teatime cupcakes.

MAKES **9**
30 MINUTES TO MAKE, PLUS
    CHILLING
20-25 MINUTES TO COOK

150G (5½OZ) UNSALTED BUTTER,
    SOFTENED
150G (5½OZ) CASTER SUGAR
3 FREE-RANGE EGGS
125G (4½OZ) SELF-RAISING FLOUR
200G (7OZ) LEFTOVER APPLE + PECAN
    CRUMBLE (PAGE 149)
SPLASH OF WHOLE MILK (OPTIONAL)

FOR THE ICING
3 TABLESPOONS CUSTARD POWDER
100ML (3½FL OZ) DOUBLE CREAM
200G (7OZ) UNSALTED BUTTER OR A MIX
    OF BUTTER, MASCARPONE, CREAM
    CHEESE (ANYTHING FIRM AND
    SPREADABLE)
125G (4½OZ) ICING SUGAR

CRUMBLE CUPCAKES

1. Preheat the oven to 180°C/fan 160°C/350°F/gas 4 and line 9 holes of a 12-hole muffin tin with paper cases.

2. In a bowl, beat the butter and caster sugar together until light and fluffy. Add the eggs, one at a time, beating before adding the next one, then add the flour and leftover crumble, reserving some to decorate. Fold together, adding a splash of milk if the mixture is too thick.

3. Dollop into the paper cases and bake for 20-25 minutes until golden and risen.

4. Meanwhile, for the icing, blend the custard powder and cream together in a small pan over a medium-low heat and cook for 2-3 minutes until you have a lovely thick paste. Set aside to cool.

5. Beat the butter (or butter, mascarpone and/or cream cheese) together with the icing sugar until fluffy. Add the cooled custard mixture and fold in. Chill for at least 30 minutes.

6. When ready to ice, spread the top of each cupcake with some of the icing. Scatter with the reserved crumble and serve.

tip To make these cupcakes from scratch, peel and core 250g (9oz) Cox apples and cook with a knob of unsalted butter, a splash of water and 1 tablespoon of caster sugar for 10 minutes, then cool. Use 50g (1¾oz) ground almonds instead of the crumble topping in the mix.

Breathe life into yesterday's crumble by transforming it into this showstopping tart.

SERVES **4**

30 MINUTES TO MAKE, PLUS
    CHILLING

50 MINUTES TO COOK

300ML (10FL OZ) DOUBLE CREAM

1 TEASPOON VANILLA EXTRACT

3 FREE-RANGE EGG YOLKS

125G (4½OZ) CASTER SUGAR

1 TABLESPOON CORNFLOUR

ABOUT 350G (12OZ) LEFTOVER APPLE +
    PECAN CRUMBLE (PAGE 149)

FOR THE PASTRY

275G (9¾OZ) PLAIN FLOUR, PLUS EXTRA
    TO DUST

180G (6¼OZ) UNSALTED BUTTER,
    CHILLED AND CUT INTO CUBES

2 TABLESPOONS CASTER SUGAR

1 FREE-RANGE EGG YOLK

APPLE + PECAN CRUMBLE TART

1. Heat the cream with the vanilla in a saucepan until almost boiling. Whisk the egg yolks with the sugar and cornflour until smooth. Pour over the hot cream and mix well, then return to the pan over a low heat and cook gently for 10–15 minutes until it thickens and coats the back of a spoon. Set aside to cool.

2. To make the tart case, put the flour and butter in a bowl and rub together with your fingertips until the mixture resembles breadcrumbs. Add the sugar followed by the egg yolk and 1–2 tablespoons of cold water and mix with a round-bladed knife. Bring together with your hands and knead briefly until smooth. Shape into a disc and chill for 10–15 minutes.

3. Preheat the oven to 200°C/fan 180°C/400°F/gas 6. Roll the pastry out on a floured surface to 2mm (⅙in) thickness and use to line a 21cm (8¼in) loose-bottomed, fluted tart tin. Line the tin with nonstick baking paper and baking beans or uncooked rice and blind bake for 15 minutes, then remove the paper and beans and bake for a further 4–5 minutes until lightly golden and dry to the touch. Reduce the temperature to 160°C/fan 140°C/325°F/gas 3.

4. Carefully remove the crumble from the top of your leftovers. Mix the fruit into the custard and pour into the tart case. Break up the crumble and scatter over the top. Bake for 30 minutes until the custard is set and the top is golden and crunchy.

tip If you don't have any leftover crumble (page 149), peel, core and roughly chop 2 small Cox apples (about 300g/10½oz) and put in a pan with a knob of unsalted butter, 20g (¾oz) caster sugar and a little splash of water. Cook for 10–15 minutes to soften slightly, then mix with the custard. Rub together 50g (1¾oz) unsalted butter with 80g (2¾oz) plain flour and 1 tablespoon of caster sugar or soft brown sugar and scatter this over the top of your tart.

Poached pears remind me of growing up as my mother would always poach pears for her dinner parties. We were never allowed to eat them until the next day, so to me they are an exotic treat and a leftover rolled into one.

SERVES **4**, PLUS LEFTOVERS
10 MINUTES TO MAKE
25 MINUTES TO COOK

STAR ANISE + HONEY POACHED PEARS

PARED ZEST OF 1 ORANGE

PARED ZEST OF 1 LEMON

2 STAR ANISE

2 TABLESPOONS CLEAR HONEY

1 VANILLA POD, SPLIT IN HALF
  LENGTHWAYS

2 X 375ML (13FL OZ) BOTTLES SWEET
  DESSERT WINE, SUCH AS SAUTERNES

6 RIPE BUT FIRM PEARS, PEELED AND
  LEFT WHOLE

1. Put the the fruit zest, star anise, honey and vanilla pod into a large saucepan, then pour over the wine and enough water to cover. Bring to the boil and simmer for 5 minutes, then add the pears and gently cook for 20-25 minutes until the pears are golden and just tender when prodded with the tip of a sharp knife.

2. Remove the pears with a slotted spoon and transfer to a heatproof bowl. Bring the syrup back to the boil, then bubble to reduce until about 500ml (18fl oz) and slightly syrupy. Cool for 10-15 minutes, then pour over the pears and leave to cool completely before serving.

ENOUGH LEFT OVER FOR:
PEAR TARTE FINE (PAGE 156)
UPSIDE DOWN PEAR + ALMOND CAKES
  (PAGE 157) »——→

A simple and elegant dessert with crisp golden pastry,
soft pears and rich almonds.

SERVES **4**
20 MINUTES TO MAKE
30 MINUTES TO COOK

30G (1OZ) UNSALTED BUTTER,
   SOFTENED

40G (1½OZ) ICING SUGAR

½ TEASPOON VANILLA EXTRACT

1 FREE-RANGE EGG, BEATEN

50G (1¾OZ) GROUND ALMONDS

½ TEASPOON CORNFLOUR

1 TABLESPOON RUM OR BRANDY

PLAIN FLOUR, TO DUST

375G (13OZ) BLOCK ALL-BUTTER PUFF
   PASTRY

1–2 LEFTOVER STAR ANISE + HONEY
   POACHED PEARS (PAGE 153)

3 TABLESPOONS APRICOT JAM

PEAR TARTE FINE

1. Preheat the oven to 200°C/fan 180°C/400°F/gas 6. Line a
baking sheet with nonstick baking paper.

2. Beat the butter, icing sugar and vanilla together until light and
fluffy. Add half the egg (reserving the other half to glaze) and beat
in, then add the almonds, cornflour and rum or brandy.

3. Roll out the pastry on a lightly floured surface until 2mm (⅙in)
thick. Cut out a circle about 22cm (8½in) in diameter. Slide on to
the lined baking sheet.

4. Use a knife to score around the edge of your pastry, about
1cm (½in) in from the edge to create a border.

5. Spread the almond cream inside the border. Slice and core
the pears, then slice into thin wedges and place on top of the
almond cream. Brush the pastry edge with the reserved beaten
egg and bake for 25–30 minutes until golden and puffed.

6. Melt the apricot jam in a pan with 2 teaspoons of water, sieve
and return to the pan, then bubble for 1–2 minutes until you have
a thick glaze. Brush all over the tart and serve.

tip If you haven't cooked the Star Anise + Honey Poached
Pears (page 153), slice 2 peeled and cored pears into thin wedges
and use raw.

As a teatime treat or with a good dollop of crème fraiche or cream as a dessert, this is the perfect way to use up leftover poached pears.

UPSIDE DOWN PEAR + ALMOND CAKES

SERVES **6**
30 MINUTES TO MAKE
40-45 MINUTES TO COOK

175G (6OZ) UNSALTED BUTTER,
  SOFTENED, PLUS EXTRA TO GREASE
100ML (3½OZ) LEFTOVER SYRUP FROM
  STAR ANISE + HONEY POACHED
  PEARS (PAGE 153)
250G (9OZ) CASTER SUGAR
2 FREE-RANGE EGGS
125G (4½OZ) SELF-RAISING FLOUR
50G (1¾OZ) GROUND ALMONDS
2 LEFTOVER STAR ANISE + HONEY
  POACHED PEARS (PAGE 153)

1. Preheat the oven to 160°C/fan 140°C/325°F/gas 3 and grease 6 x 250ml (9fl oz) ramekins.

2. Put the leftover syrup and 100g (3½oz) of the caster sugar in a saucepan and set over a low heat to melt the sugar. Increase the heat and boil until you have a golden amber caramel.

3. Meanwhile, beat the butter and remaining sugar together with a hand-held electric whisk until light and fluffy. Add the eggs one at a time, beating between each addition, then fold in the flour and ground almonds.

4. Slice the pears into little wedges and put into the bottom of the ramekins. Pour the caramel over the pears evenly. Spoon the cake mixture on top, then bake for 40–45 minutes until the sponge is risen and golden and firm to the touch. Run a knife around the edge of the ramekins, leave to stand for 2 minutes, then turn out. Leave to cool a little more, then serve warm.

tip If you haven't poached the pears (page 153), take 2 pears and peel, core and slice into wedges. Put into a pan with 150ml (5fl oz) water and 30g (1oz) caster sugar and simmer gently for about 10 minutes until just tender. Cool before using in the recipe above.

Using a mix of honey and almonds along with the more usual breadcrumbs and syrup makes this tart less tooth-achingly sweet than a simple treacle tart but no less moreish.

SERVES **4**, PLUS LEFTOVERS
30 MINUTES TO MAKE, PLUS
 CHILLING
1 HOUR **10** MINUTES TO COOK

STICKY ALMOND + HONEY TART

FOR THE PASTRY
200G (7OZ) PLAIN FLOUR, PLUS EXTRA
 TO DUST
PINCH OF SEA SALT
110G (3¾OZ) COLD UNSALTED BUTTER,
 CUT INTO CUBES

FOR THE FILLING
100G (3½OZ) SOFT WHITE
 BREADCRUMBS
80G (2¾OZ) GROUND ALMONDS
500G (1LB 2OZ) GOLDEN SYRUP
250G (9OZ) CLEAR HONEY
GRATED ZEST OF 1 LEMON
2 FREE-RANGE EGGS, BEATEN
3 TABLESPOONS DOUBLE CREAM
DOUBLE CREAM OR ICE CREAM,
 TO SERVE

1. To make the pastry, put the flour and salt in a bowl, add the butter and rub together with your fingertips until it resembles breadcrumbs. Add enough cold water to just start to bring the mixture together with the rounded blade of a knife.

2. Bring the pastry together with your hands and knead briefly until smooth. Roll out on a lightly floured surface and line a 23 x 3cm (9 x ¼in) deep, fluted tart tin. Prick with a fork and chill for 30 minutes.

3. Preheat the oven to 200°C/fan 180°C/400°F/gas 6 and put a baking sheet in to heat up. Line the pastry case with nonstick baking paper and baking beans or uncooked rice. Bake for 15 minutes, then remove the paper and baking beans or rice and return to the oven for 5 minutes until lightly golden. Set aside and reduce the temperature to 160°C/fan 140°C/325°F/gas 3.

4. For the filling, put the breadcrumbs and almonds in a bowl. In a pan, melt the syrup and honey until runny, then add the lemon zest. Mix well, then add the eggs and cream and mix again. Pour this mixture over the breadcrumbs and almonds and leave to stand for 5 minutes until it starts to swell and absorb the liquid.

5. Pour evenly into the pastry case and bake for 45–50 minutes until golden brown and set. Cool in the tin for 10–15 minutes, then transfer to a plate and serve with cream or ice cream.

ENOUGH LEFT OVER FOR:
SEMIFREDDO SLICE (PAGE 160)
STUFFED BAKED APPLES (PAGE 162) »⟶

The ultimate lazy way to make ice cream – no churning, just a little whisk and a good freeze.

3 LARGE FREE-RANGE EGGS, SEPARATED
90G (3¼OZ) CASTER SUGAR
400ML (14FL OZ) DOUBLE CREAM,
   MASCARPONE OR A MIXTURE
250G (9OZ) LEFTOVER STICKY ALMOND
   + HONEY TART (PAGE 159)

SEMIFREDDO SLICE

1. Line a 900g (2lb) loaf tin (or any other similar-sized tin) with clingfilm, leaving some hanging over the edge.

2. Whisk the egg yolks with the sugar until really light and fluffy and voluminous. Add the cream or mascarpone or mixture and beat until billowy.

3. Whisk the egg whites in a clean bowl until holding stiff peaks, then gently fold into the egg yolk mixture.

4. Break the leftover tart into small chunks and fold these through the mixture, being careful not to knock out any air. Carefully pour into the lined tin, covering with the excess clingfilm. Freeze for at least 12 hours.

5. About 30 minutes before you want to serve, remove from the freezer. Slice with a hot knife and serve.

tip You could be really naughty and use a bought treacle tart for this recipe, or crumble up shortbread biscuits and coat them in honey, then stir them into the semifreddo if you don't have any leftover tart (page 159) to use up.

Sometimes the most simple desserts are the best, and soft, yielding baked apples are pretty hard to beat. But they are even better with a sticky almond and honey tart centre.

SERVES **6**
15 MINUTES TO MAKE
30-40 MINUTES TO COOK

150-200G (5½-7OZ) LEFTOVER STICKY
  ALMOND + HONEY TART (PAGE 159)
50G (1¾OZ) UNSALTED BUTTER,
  SOFTENED
PINCH OF GROUND ALLSPICE
GRATING OF NUTMEG
6 APPLES, SUCH AS AMBROSIA, COX
  OR OTHER EATING APPLES
CREAM, CRÈME FRAÎCHE,
  MASCARPONE OR ICE CREAM,
  TO SERVE

STUFFED BAKED APPLES

1. Preheat the oven to 180°C/fan 160°C/350°F/gas 4. Break the leftover tart up with a fork. Mix with the butter and the spices.

2. Core the apples and make a thin score around their middles. Stuff them with the honey tart mixture, then stand in a baking tray. Bake for 30–40 minutes until the apples are tender. Serve with cream, crème fraîche, mascarpone or ice cream.

tip Without any leftover tart (page 159) you can fill your apples with a mix of oats and shortbread. Melt a knob of unsalted butter in a pan, add 150g (5½oz) oats that have been lightly toasted in a low oven and 2 tablespoons of golden syrup or clear honey and simmer together gently. Crumble in a shortbread biscuit before using to stuff the apples.

One of my favourite London bakeries is Fabrique – a Nordic bakery which makes wonderful cinnamon and cardamom buns. This recipe is my homage to their wonderful pastries.

CARDAMOM + CINNAMON BUNS

MAKES ABOUT **18**
1 HOUR TO MAKE, PLUS RISING
15-20 MINUTES TO COOK

500ML (18FL OZ) WHOLE MILK
125G (4½OZ) UNSALTED BUTTER, CUT
   INTO PIECES
800G (1LB 12OZ) STRONG WHITE BREAD
   FLOUR, PLUS EXTRA TO DUST
1 TEASPOON SEA SALT
7G (¼OZ) SACHET ACTIVE DRIED
   YEAST
90G (3¼OZ) CASTER SUGAR
1 FREE-RANGE EGG

FOR THE FILLING
75G (2¾OZ) UNSALTED BUTTER,
   SOFTENED
1 TABLESPOON GROUND CINNAMON
½ TABLESPOON GROUND CARDAMOM
75G (2¾OZ) CASTER SUGAR

FOR THE SUGAR SYRUP
100G (3½OZ) CASTER SUGAR

1. Heat the milk with the butter in a saucepan until the butter has melted. Set aside until it is just lukewarm.

2. Tip the flour and salt into a bowl. Mix the yeast and sugar in a separate bowl with a couple of tablespoons of warm water and leave to stand for 10 minutes until frothy.

3. Add the milk, butter and yeast to the flour and mix together until you have a soft, slightly sticky dough. Tip out on to a lightly floured surface and knead for 10 minutes. Return to a clean bowl, cover with oiled clingfilm and leave in a warm place until doubled in size.

4. Beat the butter, spices and sugar together until spreadable.

5. Turn the dough out and punch down with your fingertips, then roll into a rectangle about 30 x 40cm (12 x 16in) on a piece of nonstick baking paper or a clean tea towel. Spread with the butter, then roll up along the long side, using the paper or tea towel to help you. Slice into 2cm (¾in) thick slices.

6. Place the buns, cut-side up, on a lightly oiled baking sheet. Cover with oiled clingfilm and set aside for 30 minutes until doubled in size. Preheat the oven to 220°C/fan 200°C/425°F/gas 7. Mix the egg with a little water and glaze the buns all over, then bake for 15-20 minutes until golden and risen. Bubble the sugar and 100ml (3½fl oz) water together to form a light sugar syrup. Brush over the warm buns and leave to cool before serving.

ENOUGH LEFT OVER FOR:
CARDAMOM BUN + CREAM PUDDING (PAGE 166)
PAIN PERDU (PAGE 167) »——→

A soft, silky pillow of a pudding, this is so much more than an average bread and butter pudding.

SERVES 4

SERVES 4
10 MINUTES TO MAKE,
   PLUS SOAKING
30 MINUTES TO COOK

400ML (14FL OZ) WHOLE MILK OR A MIX
   OF MILK AND CREAM
2 FREE-RANGE EGG YOLKS
1 TABLESPOON CASTER SUGAR, PLUS
   EXTRA TO SPRINKLE
UNSALTED BUTTER, TO GREASE
4 LEFTOVER CARDAMOM + CINNAMON
   BUNS (PAGE 163)

CARDAMOM BUN + CREAM PUDDING

1. Preheat the oven to 180°C/fan 160°C/350°F/gas 4.

2. Heat the milk (or milk and cream) in a saucepan until just boiling. Remove from the heat and set aside.

3. Beat the egg yolks and sugar in a heatproof bowl, then pour the hot milk over the top and stir well. Grease a 1.2-litre (2-pint) ovenproof dish with butter.

4. Tear the leftover buns into pieces and arrange them in the dish, then pour over the custard. Leave to soak for 15–20 minutes.

5. Bake for 25–30 minutes until softly set and golden. Scatter with caster sugar and serve.

tip If you haven't made the Cardamom + Cinnamon Buns (page 163), you could use slices of brioche or croissant instead and add a little ground cardamom and cinnamon to the custard.

This recipe is a wonderful way to turn a few day-old buns into a delicious breakfast.

SERVES **4**
15 MINUTES TO MAKE
10 MINUTES TO COOK

PAIN PERDU

3 FREE-RANGE EGGS

175ML (6FL OZ) WHOLE MILK

50G (1¾OZ) UNSALTED BUTTER

3-4 LEFTOVER CARDAMOM +
   CINNAMON BUNS (PAGE 163), HALVED

MAPLE SYRUP OR CLEAR HONEY AND
   DOUBLE CREAM, CRÈME FRAÎCHE OR
   MASCARPONE, TO SERVE

1. Whisk the eggs and the milk together in a bowl. Melt half the butter in a frying pan. Dip half the leftover buns in the eggy mixture and fry for 2 minutes on each side until set. Remove to a plate. Wipe the pan with kitchen paper and repeat with the remaining butter and buns.

2. Serve with maple syrup or honey and dollops of cream, crème fraîche or mascarpone.

tip Use slices of brioche instead of the Cardamom + Cinnamon Buns (page 163) and add a pinch of ground cardamom and cinnamon to the egg mixture.

The only things my granny could cook were meatloaf and a wonderful chocolate mousse. The latter always went wrong but somehow was more delicious for it. I've never managed to recreate her mousse, but this is my version in her honour.

RICH CHOCOLATE MOUSSE

MAKES **8**

20 MINUTES TO MAKE, PLUS CHILLING

200G (7OZ) DARK CHOCOLATE, APPROX. 70 PER CENT COCOA SOLIDS

150ML (5FL OZ) DOUBLE CREAM

3 LARGE FREE-RANGE EGGS, SEPARATED

45G (1¾OZ) CASTER SUGAR

1. Break the chocolate into small pieces and put in a large heatproof bowl. Heat the cream to almost boiling, then pour over the chocolate. Stir to mix, then add the egg yolks.

2. Whisk the egg whites in a clean bowl until they form soft peaks, then gradually whisk in the sugar until you have a glossy light meringue.

3. Mix a quarter of the meringue into the chocolate mixture to loosen it, then very carefully fold in the rest, being careful not to knock out too much of the air. Spoon into 8 x 150ml (5fl oz) glasses and chill for at least 2 hours before serving.

ENOUGH LEFT OVER FOR:
MINI CHOC 'N' NUT ICE CREAMS (PAGE 170)
CHOCOLATE FRIDGE CAKE (PAGE 171) »——→

The idea for these came from my love of the retro ice cream 'the chocolate feast' – so this provides a bit of childhood nostalgia for a sunny day.

MINI CHOC 'N' NUT ICE CREAMS

MAKES **6**
10 MINUTES TO MAKE
3 HOURS TO FREEZE

200G (7OZ) LEFTOVER RICH CHOCOLATE
  MOUSSE (PAGE 169)
200G (7OZ) DARK CHOCOLATE, APPROX.
  70 PER CENT COCOA SOLIDS, BROKEN
  INTO PIECES
50G (1¾OZ) TOASTED HAZELNUTS,
  CHOPPED

1. Use a mini ice cream scoop or a spoon dipped in hot water to scoop out balls or quenelles of the leftover chocolate mousse. Put on to a small baking sheet lined with nonstick baking paper, then freeze until solid – this will take about 2½ hours.

2. Melt the chocolate in a heatproof bowl over a pan of barely simmering water, then set aside.

3. Bring the frozen chocolate balls out of the freezer and stand on a wire rack over a baking sheet. Pour over the slightly cooled melted chocolate and very quickly scatter with the chopped hazelnuts. Return to the freezer to solidify before serving.

Fridge cake reminds me of my best friend Cat who adores this chilled sweet treat. I once made it for her birthday in a battered old frying pan, which was the only vessel we had to hand.

MAKES **18** SQUARES
5 MINUTES TO MAKE
10 MINUTES TO CHILL

CHOCOLATE FRIDGE CAKE

200G (7OZ) LEFTOVER RICH
  CHOCOLATE MOUSSE (PAGE 169)
2 TABLESPOONS GOLDEN SYRUP
150G (5½OZ) MIX OF YUMMY BITS,
  SUCH AS BROKEN BISCUITS,
  MARSHMALLOWS, DRIED FRUITS,
  HONEYCOMB AND NUTS
  (ANYTHING YOU LIKE!)

1. Put the chocolate mousse in a bowl, add the golden syrup, then stir in the remaining ingredients.

2. Pour into a small cake or loaf tin lined with nonstick baking paper and chill until solid. Cut into cubes and serve.

tip If you don't have any leftovers, use shop-bought chocolate mousse or you can melt 75g (2¾oz) chocolate with 75ml (5 tablespoons) double cream to form a ganache. Leave it to cool a little, then add the golden syrup and remaining ingredients and continue as above.

INDEX

UK/US GLOSSARY

aubergine – eggplant
baking tray – baking sheet
beetroot – beet
biscuit – cookie
broad beans – fava beans
caster sugar – superfine sugar
cornflour – corn starch
clingfilm – plastic wrap
chips – fries
coriander – cilantro
courgette – zucchini
double cream – heavy cream
frying pan – skillet
grill – broil/broiler
icing sugar – confectioners' sugar
jam – jelly
mince – ground meat
prawns – shrimp
plain flour – all-purpose flour
rocket – arugula
self-raising flour – self-rising flour
starter – appetizer
strong white bread flour – strong flour

THANK YOU

This book is so much more than a book on leftovers cooking. As a subject, leftovers are quite a tricky thing to write about, being in their nature something that you cannot predict you will have. The way it made most sense to me was to write a book about the way I cook. Always cooking a little bit more than I probably need, and keeping a well-stocked fridge and store cupboard for fridge-raiding suppers, which have always been my favourite. I love no-rules cooking and this book explores how to use the bounty in your own kitchen to come up with some truly fun and different uses for leftovers.

I couldn't possibly have done this book on my own and there are so many wonderful people who have played a part in how beautiful and simple it is.

Firstly to my Moomin Mama – who taught me that everything is worth saving, from a single sausage to a small bowl of rice or a spoonful of sauce. Nothing is wasted in her kitchen and her love and passion for food has infiltrated my very soul.

To my dream-team girlies: Ted and her beautiful pictures, her talent for making everything look a million dollars is staggering, and my Noobs, the best sister and partner in crime, who knows me and my recipes inside out and always knows how best to make them shine with her wonderful props and scenes. Without you ladies this book would never be as perfect. Thank you, as always, from the bottom of my heart.

To my gorge assistants, Katie and April. The biggest thanks and hugs to you both for your amazing kitchen skills and for keeping things shipshape and running smoothly. I truly would be lost without you!

Huge thanks to Vicky, my editor, and the wonderful Kyle for allowing me to write such a dreamy book and turn the subject of leftovers into one of excitement and beauty. Thank you for putting up with me and producing such a wonderful book.

Thank you to all my family and friends for your endless tasting and re-tasting of dishes, and for all your support and love.